St. Paul

STEWARD OF THE MYSTERIES

A BIBLE STUDY GUIDE FOR CATHOLICS

ST. PAUL

STEWARD OF THE MYSTERIES

A BIBLE STUDY GUIDE FOR CATHOLICS

FR. MITCH PACWA, S.J.

Birmingham Catholic Press, Inc.
Birmingham, Alabama

Our Sunday Visitor Publishing Division
Our Sunday Visitor, Inc.
Huntington, Indiana

Imprimi Potest
Very Reverend Edward W. Schmidt, S.J.
Provincial of the Chicago Province of the Society of Jesus

Nihil Obstat
Very Reverend Kevin M. Bazzel, J.C.L.
Chancellor
Diocese of Birmingham in Alabama

Imprimatur
✠ Robert J. Baker, S.T.D.
Bishop of Birmingham in Alabama
February 26, 2008

The *Nihil Obstat* and *Imprimatur* are official declarations that a book is free from doctrinal or moral error. It is not implied that those who have granted the *Nihil Obstat* and *Imprimatur* agree with the contents, opinions, or statements expressed.

Our Sunday Visitor Publishing Division
Our Sunday Visitor, Inc.
200 Noll Plaza
Huntington, IN 46750

ISBN: 978-1-59276-420-4 (Inventory No. T555)
LCCN: 2008924836

Cover design: Lindsey Luken
Cover art: The Crosiers
Interior design: Sherri L. Hoffman

PRINTED IN THE UNITED STATES OF AMERICA

To my brother
Paul Pacwa
(November 11, 1952–January 12, 2008)

✠

May he rest in peace

CONTENTS

PREFACE

During my installation as bishop of Birmingham on October 2, 2007, in the Cathedral of St. Paul, I mentioned in my homily that Pope Benedict XVI had invited the Universal Church to take part in a Jubilee Year honoring St. Paul, on the 2,000th anniversary of his birth. The yearlong celebration would begin with the Solemnity of Sts. Peter and Paul, June 29, 2008, and conclude one year later on the same feast day.

Following the Mass, Father Mitch Pacwa, S. J., approached me with a suggestion to do something special, honoring the saint who is the patron of our cathedral and our diocese. After some discussion, Father Mitch agreed to write a Bible study guide that would help people come to a greater understanding of the sacraments that we Catholics celebrate throughout our lives as followers of Christ.

St. Paul, as you will see in this study guide, had much to say about the sacraments. Being both a very insightful scholar of Sacred Scripture and the writings of St. Paul and a very capable commentator on our Catholic faith, reaching millions of people through twice-weekly programs on the Eternal Word Television Network (EWTN), Father Pacwa provides us with a broad spectrum of St. Paul's teachings on the Sacraments of Baptism, Penance (Reconciliation), Confirmation, the Holy Eucharist, Holy Orders, and Matrimony. Father Mitch offers us what he has gleaned from years of study and prayer.

Along the way, St. Paul's vibrant teaching comes alive for us, and we are eager to hear more of what St. Paul has to offer us. Hopefully, Father Mitch's commentaries will encourage us to read all the letters of St. Paul in the course of the Year of St. Paul.

My prayer is that the Holy Spirit will work in our lives, as that Spirit worked in the life of St. Paul, helping us to cherish our great faith in the Lord, present in the sacraments of our Church, and enabling us to be witnesses of the love of Christ in the world in which we live.

MOST REVEREND ROBERT J. BAKER, S.T.D.
Bishop of Birmingham in Alabama
Feast of the Conversion of St. Paul
January 25, 2008

HOW TO USE THIS STUDY GUIDE IN A GROUP

This is an interactive study guide. It can be read with profit either alone or as part of a group Bible study. Below are suggestions for the use of this book in a group.

WHAT YOU WILL NEED FOR EVERY SESSION

- This study guide
- A Bible
- A notebook

- **Before Session 1, members of the group are encouraged to read the Introduction and Session 1 and to complete all the exercises in both.** They should bring this study guide with them to the group session.

- **Begin the session with prayer** (for example, A Prayer to the Apostle Paul, on page 95).

- **Invite one person in the group to read one of the passages from St. Paul included in this session's material.**

- **Allow five minutes of silent reflection on the passage.** This allows the group to quiet their inner thoughts and to center themselves on the lesson to be discussed on St. Paul.

- **Catechesis:** Give all members a chance to share some point that they have learned, either about St. Paul or the sacrament discussed in the material. Was this something new or a new insight into something? Was there anything that raised a question? (Allow fifteen to twenty minutes for this.)

- **Discussion:** Use the discussion questions at the end of the session chapter to begin a deeper grasp of the material covered in the session. (Allow fifteen to twenty minutes for this).

- **Conclusion:** Have all members of the group summarize the key concepts they learned about St. Paul and the sacrament discussed in the session. Assign the next session as homework, to be completed before the next group session.

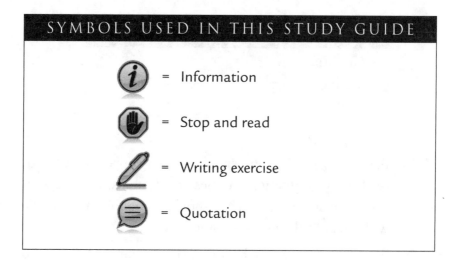

SYMBOLS USED IN THIS STUDY GUIDE

= Information

= Stop and read

= Writing exercise

= Quotation

Introduction

ST. PAUL: A CATHOLIC APOSTLE

In St. Paul's First Letter to the Corinthians, the apostle wrote that he wanted people to consider him and his fellow missionaries as "stewards of the mysteries of God" (1 Cor 4:1). The term "mysteries" has a range of meanings, including those things which had remained hidden since the foundation of the world, but were now revealed by Christ (Eph 1:4; 3:9; Col 1:26; 1 Cor 2:7), and the mystery of why the Jewish people will not accept Jesus as their Messiah until the full number of Gentiles become Christian (Rom 11:25). In the Eastern churches, both Eastern-rite Catholic churches and Orthodox churches, "mysteries" is the term for the seven signs instituted by Christ to effect and signify holiness and righteousness. The Vulgate (St. Jerome's Latin translation of the Bible) uses the word *sacramentum* to translate the Greek word *musterion* — that is, "mystery." It is in this last sense that this book speaks of St. Paul as a "steward of the

---

"STEWARDS OF GOD"

The Greek word for "steward" is *oikonomos*. This normally has the sense of an overseer of a house (*oikos* in Greek) who oversees giving the provisions for the members of the house. He typically reported directly to the master of the house (*oikodespotes* in Greek), to whom he had to give a strict account for his task (Lk 12:42-48; 16:1-9; Mt 20:8-16; Jn 2:8-10). Outside Scripture, the word was also used for the treasurer of a city and for Temple officials. St. Paul will use the term only in 1 Corinthians 4:1-2 and in Titus 1:7, in reference to bishops who are "the stewards of God."

mysteries of God," in order to use this phrase as a jumping-off point to discuss the apostle's teaching on the sacraments.

Receiving the sacraments is a defining characteristic of Catholic life: newborn babies are baptized; young children make their first confession and receive their first Holy Communion. Later in childhood, they receive Confirmation. As adults, Catholics may enter Holy Matrimony or be ordained to the priesthood. Sinners confess throughout their lives, and the sick receive the Anointing of the Sick. The dying receive last rites, which, when possible, include the celebration of three sacraments — Penance, Anointing of the Sick, and Holy Communion. One cannot help but notice that each sacrament includes some specific actions — pouring water, telling one's sins, receiving Holy Communion, having hands laid upon one's head, or being anointed. In addition, the actions include ceremonies where Scripture is read, prayers are recited, and the recipients of each sacrament make professions of faith and commitments to God and one another. These words confer a set of rich meanings to these otherwise simple actions. Neither these specific actions nor the accompanying words are — nor can be — omitted for a sacrament to be true and effective in one's life. Catholics willingly receive these sacraments, and they find tremendous personal peace in them and communal celebration. They even find, during severe crises, that the sacraments are worth dying for.

This is why Catholics cherish the gift that Christ conveys to his people through these mysteries. The sacraments are not merely precepts of a Church that some might argue are irrelevant distractions at best or construed fabrications at worst. Rather, they are biblically founded means that convey Christ's efficacious grace upon his Church, signifying the spiritual realities they represent through physical signs and actions. It is none other than St. Paul of Tarsus himself who most prominently extols the sacraments in the New Testament after the resurrection of Christ.

This study will highlight St. Paul's teachings about the sacraments, which are interwoven throughout his letters. His message about the sacraments is not limited to one letter or some small aspect of his teaching. Rather, the sacraments, and the teaching about the Church itself, belong to the very essence of his teaching. St. Paul is a truly Catholic apostle, as is evidenced by the prominence of his epistles among the readings at Mass on Sundays and weekdays alike. Catholics need to immerse themselves in St. Paul's writings in order to better understand the teachings of their Church.

Before beginning this Bible study of St. Paul and his teaching on the sacraments, you might want to take a little time to familiarize yourself with St. Paul.

THE APOSTLE PAUL

St. Paul has been a controversial figure throughout history. He was born in a peaceful enough city — Tarsus, in Asia Minor (modern Turkey). His parents belonged to the Israelite tribe of Benjamin and held Roman citizenship (which included civil rights), into which Saul (his Jewish name) was born and which he would need to claim during the frequent crises of his adult life (Acts 22:25-28). However, as members of the Pharisee party of Jews (Phil 3:5), they sent Saul to study in Jerusalem under Rabbi Gamaliel (Acts 22:3), a scholar so highly esteemed that when he died it was written that "the glory of the Law ceased and purity and abstinence died" (Mishnah, Sotah 9:15).

Saul excelled among the rabbinical students of his time (Gal 1:14), which apparently motivated him to actively persecute the early Church in the A.D. 30s. He participated in the execution of St. Stephen, the first martyr (Acts 7:58; 8:1), and then in the subsequent persecution of the whole Church. With authorization from the chief priests, he went to arrest Christians in Damascus.

However, on the road he was stopped by a vision of light that asked him, "Saul, Saul, why do you persecute me?" Saul did not recognize the voice and was then told, "I am Jesus, whom you are persecuting" (Acts 9:4, 5). Upon Jesus' instructions, Saul, now blinded by the apparition, was led into Damascus, where he was baptized by Ananias (Acts 9:17-18).

Saul began preaching about Jesus so fervently that his life was at risk (Acts 9:22-25). He went to Jerusalem, where again his preaching evoked threats against his life (Acts 9:26-30).

 Stop here and read Paul's account of the suffering he endured to preach the Gospel, in **2 Corinthians 11:21-29**.

From there he went to Tarsus, where he remained until Barnabas called for him to help teach new Gentile converts in the city of Antioch (Acts 11:25-26). Christian prophets were inspired to have the Church send Saul and Barnabas on a mission to other Gentile cities and regions, first to Cyprus and Asia Minor, and on a second trip to Asia Minor and Europe. A third journey followed, with a probable fourth trip, which occurs after the Acts of the Apostles ends its history of the early Church in A.D. 62, with Paul under house arrest in Rome awaiting trial by Nero.

Both the Acts of the Apostles (written by St. Paul's traveling companion, St. Luke) and Paul's own letters frequently mention the arrests, beatings, and riots caused by Paul's preaching throughout the Mediterranean world. Later in history, St. Paul's epistles would continue to cause controversy and strife, particularly during the Protestant Reformation and later. Some people even think that Paul is for Protestants and that Catholicism is based on other parts of the New Testament, but as you will see in this study, this clearly is not the case.

ST. PAUL'S CRISES

 Look up the passages listed in the table below and then enter what "crisis" St. Paul had to deal with in that passage.

PASSAGE	CRISIS
Acts 17-18	
Acts 19:23-34	
Acts 21:27-36	
Acts 22:17-26	
2 Corinthians 6:3-10	
2 Corinthians 11:23-28	
2 Timothy 1:8-12	
2 Timothy 3:10-13	

Session 1

TO BE ONE WITH CHRIST

St. Paul on Baptism

CONSIDER

St. Paul wrote some significant teachings on Baptism, but he also experienced it as a recipient and as a minister of it, as witnessed in the Acts of the Apostles.

 Stop here and read the account of St. Paul's conversion aloud. You'll find it in **Acts 9:1-9**.

Three days after Saul had been blinded, a Christian named Ananias saw Christ in a vision, and the Lord told him to visit Saul, who had also received a vision preparing him for Ananias' visit. Though Ananias knew that Saul had come to Damascus to arrest the Christians, he addressed him as "brother." Ananias laid hands upon Saul so that he might see again and be full of the Holy Spirit. Saul was able to see immediately and was baptized (Acts 9:17-19).

Paul the Apostle would go throughout Asia Minor and other regions of the Roman Empire preaching the Gospel of Jesus Christ and baptizing those who accepted his teaching:

- The first Christian believer in Europe was Lydia, whose heart was opened to accept Paul's teaching in Philippi, and she and her household were baptized (Acts 16:13-15).

- In the same city of Philippi, Paul was later jailed for casting a demon out of a slave girl. An earthquake damaged the jail, and the warden attempted to commit suicide because he thought the prisoners had escaped. When Paul assured him that all were still there, he asked: "Sirs, what must I do to be saved?" Paul answered, "Believe in the Lord Jesus and you and your whole house will be saved." After teaching him the faith, Paul baptized the warden and his whole household (Acts 16:25-34).

- Months later, in Corinth, Paul baptized Crispus and many others who believed in the Lord (Acts 18:8; see also

CHRONOLOGY OF ST. PAUL'S LETTERS

The order of St. Paul's epistles in the New Testament is dependent, first, upon the length of each letter (beginning with the longest, Romans) and, second, by the audience (to a community — that is, from Romans through 2 Thessalonians; and to individuals — from 1 Timothy through Philemon), and not the chronology when the letter was actually composed. Though scholars debate and disagree about some letters, there is a general consensus about many of them:

- **1 and 2 Thessalonians** were written from Corinth around A.D. 51.
- **1 and 2 Corinthians** were written in Ephesus about the year 55.
- **Romans** was composed about the year 56; most scholars believe that Galatians came before Romans, but the year is highly disputed.
- **Philippians**, **Ephesians**, **Colossians**, and **Philemon** may have been written from imprisonment in Caesarea Maritima between the years 58 and 60.
- **1 and 2 Timothy** and **Titus** seem to come from the early to mid-60s.

1 Cor 1:14-16, which mentions baptizing the same Crispus, plus Gaius and Stephanas).

- A more interesting occasion occurs in Ephesus (Acts 19:1-17). Verses 1-4 indicate that John's baptism did not have the power to communicate the Holy Spirit, which is consistent with the Gospel reports of John's ministry: Jesus, not John, would baptize in the Spirit (Mt 3:11; Mk 1:8; Lk 3:16; Jn 1:33; Acts 1:5; 11:16). Upon hearing Paul's clarification of the difference in power between John's baptism and the more powerful baptism into Jesus Christ, the twelve men were baptized in the name of Jesus. Then Paul laid hands on them and the Holy Spirit came down upon them, and they began to speak in tongues and prophesy.

Having seen how St. Luke describes some of Paul's experiences of Baptism, let us turn to his teaching on it in his letters, or epistles. We will present this teaching in the chronological order of Paul's composition of the epistles.

INVESTIGATE

ST. PAUL'S IDEAS ON THE CHURCH

 What does St. Paul teach about the Church? Look up these passages and jot down some key ideas presented in each letter of how St. Paul defines the Church.

PASSAGE	KEY CONCEPTS
1 Corinthians 12-14	***Example:*** Body of Christ, made up of many members; hierarchy; love; everything done for edification, etc.

Ephesians 2:11-22	
Ephesians 3:8-12	
Ephesians 4:4-14	
Colossians 1:15-20	
1 Timothy 3:14-16	

STUDY

St. Paul's first teaching on Baptism appears in 1 Corinthians 6, where he addresses the Christian believers on their moral life and the effects Baptism should have on it:

> [9]Do you not know that the unrighteous will not inherit the kingdom of God? Do not be deceived; neither the immoral, nor idolaters, nor adulterers, nor homosexuals, [10]nor thieves, nor the greedy, nor drunkards, nor revilers, nor robbers will inherit the kingdom of God. [11]And such were some of you. But you were washed, you were sanctified, you were justified in the name of the Lord Jesus Christ and in the Spirit of our God. (1 Cor 6:9-11)

The beginning of 1 Corinthians 6 is St. Paul's rebuke to the Christians who are pressing lawsuits against each other. On the one hand, he exhorts them to be willing to suffer wrongs rather than take each other to secular courts (6:1-8); on the other hand, he warns Christians to avoid those vices — especially various forms of sexual immorality and greed — lest they become disqualified to inherit the kingdom of God. These sins, particularly the sexual ones, had made Corinth internationally infamous. In fact, to call someone a "Corinthian" was to insult them with an accusation of sexual deviancy or profligacy.

In contrast to this warning, St. Paul reminds the Christians of their true identity as linked to their baptism. The phrase "You were washed" refers to having received this sacrament. Most importantly he adds, "You were sanctified, you were justified," in direct connection with being washed in Baptism. Being made holy and righteous before God is elsewhere connected with faith (see, for example, Gal 2-3 and Rom 3-4). However, here it is also linked with Baptism. St. Paul asserts that this spiritual transformation occurs with this sacrament, so as to motivate the Christians to cease acting like their Corinthian neighbors and to live in a way that avoids sin so as to be able to inherit the kingdom of God. However, he does not explain here how Baptism has such spiritual power; he will do so in Galatians and Romans.

St. Paul never threatens his readers with hellfire; he simply warns them about the possibility of not inheriting heaven, a threat from which one can conclude the alternative fate.

Later in the same letter (1 Cor 12:12-26), St. Paul offers another aspect of Baptism in its connection with the whole Body of Christ. The main point of the passage is in verse 12: "For just as the body is one and has many members, and all the members of the body, though many, are one body, so it is with Christ." This begins one of St. Paul's most profound insights: the Church is the Body of Christ; Christ is the Head. He learned this truth at his conversion, when Jesus asked: "Saul, Saul, why do you persecute me?" (Acts 9:4). Jesus did not challenge Saul about persecuting "the Christians" or "the Church." Rather, to persecute the Church meant persecuting Jesus himself. Paul learned in this encounter precisely what the disciples had heard from Jesus during his public ministry: Jesus radically identifies himself with his disciples.

INVESTIGATE

A RADICAL IDENTITY

 Before proceeding, take a moment to look up these passages from the Gospels and discuss how Christ's teaching shows Jesus' radical identification with his followers. How does this teaching match what St. Paul both experienced and taught about the Church?

PASSAGE	KEY CONCEPTS
Matthew 18:20	
Matthew 25:40, 45	
John 15:1-6	

STUDY

Having introduced the issue, Paul then explains how the Christians become members of the Body of Christ. "For by one Spirit we were all baptized into one body — Jews or Greeks, slaves or free — and all were made to drink of one Spirit" (1 Cor 12:13). Clearly, one aspect of Baptism is that it brings us into the Body of Christ, effecting this radical identification Jesus makes with each and every Christian. It also assumes that there is only one Body of Christ, not many, thereby requiring the Christian to join that one body and no other. The remainder of the passage (1 Cor 12:14-20) teaches that within the one Body of Christ a wonderful diversity of gifts completes the whole; no one individual can have all the gifts. Rather, the members of the Body of Christ are mutually interdependent, even as they are dependent on their relationship with the Person, Jesus Christ. St. Paul had learned this from his own conversion, when his baptism led to membership in the Church.

The opening verses of Galatians 3:23-29 treat the main topic of Paul's Letter to the Galatians — namely, the relationship between Jewish law (specifically, the commandment to circumcise) and the righteousness that comes through faith in Jesus Christ. The relevant point here is that St. Paul indicates that the role of the Law is similar to a pedagogue or "custodian," setting limits on human behavior until the time of full inheritance begins. However, Christians live in a time when Christ has come, opening them to faith in him and therefore to a filial relationship with God.

Galatians 3:27-29 offers another example of Paul's teachings on Baptism. "For as many of you as were baptized into Christ have put on Christ" (v. 27). This verse assumes that Baptism has the

DOES BAPTISM MEAN "IMMERSION"?

The Greek verb *baptizo*, from which "baptism" is derived, can have a variety of nuances, ranging from "immerse," to "be waterlogged" (of a sunken ship), to "sprinkle," or "wash." 1 Corinthians 10:2 poses a most interesting use of the verb. The people of Israel were "baptized into Moses in the cloud and in the sea," a reference to the Exodus. Remember that the only persons to be immersed at the Red Sea were the Egyptians; the Israelites went through "dry-shod" and never got wet. Baptism does not always mean "immerse."

power to envelop us in Christ, as in clothing. Whereas, in 1 Corinthians 12:13, Baptism makes us a member of the Body of Christ, here the image is one of being clothed with Christ, as if with a mantle or other garment. Both images have a form of incorporation into Christ as their point. Baptism has a mysterious power to unite a person with Christ.

"There is neither Jew nor Greek, there is neither slave nor free, there is neither male nor female; for you are all one in Christ Jesus" (Gal 3:28). The Law emphasized the distinctiveness of Israel from the Gentiles, highlighting God's election of Abraham and his descendants from among all the other people of the world. Certainly, Gentiles could convert to Israel by receiving circumcision (for males), but a slave convert needed three generations after the conversion for his family to be considered fully Jewish (females could not receive the sign of the covenant, and were a case apart from the men).

In contrast, Christian Baptism did not distinguish between Jewish pedigree, slave or free status, or gender. Any and all of these groups could be as baptized as the other. This shows how Jesus is the Lord of the whole world, helping Abraham and his seed fulfill their original vocation to be a blessing to all the families of the earth (Gen 12:2-3). Therefore, Baptism brings a profound unity among all people who receive it. As in 1 Corinthians 12, where baptism into the Body of Christ effects a unity within the whole Church because of each member's union with Jesus Christ the Head, so also, here, Baptism effects a unity among all peoples, at all levels of social status, and between the genders.

Finally, in Galatians 3:29, St. Paul says that to belong to Christ by Baptism makes us sharers in the promises to Abraham: "And if you are Christ's, then you are Abraham's offspring, heirs according to promise." We "inherit" the promise because we are baptized into Jesus, the Son of God and the "seed" of Abraham. God promised Abraham that he would become a blessing for all nations (Gen

12:2-3) and that his seed would inherit the land (Gen 15:5 — "Look toward heaven, and number the stars, if you are able to number them." Then he said to him, "So shall your descendants be."). Now Paul recognizes Jesus Christ as that seed who fulfills the promise of Genesis 15:5. Since Baptism effects a union with Jesus, making us one in him, therefore Baptism joins us to the promises given to Abraham. This is so powerful a union that we belong to Christ and become heirs of the promise. St. Paul further explains that we are adopted by God because of our union with Christ in Baptism. Therefore we receive inheritance of eternal life (Gal 4:4-7; Rom 8:14-17). Of course, Baptism is not the final stage of union with Christ, as Romans 8:16-17 makes clear:

St. Paul uses the image of being clothed in Christ elsewhere:

- **Ephesians 4:24**
- **Ephesians 6:13-17**

> [16]It is the Spirit himself bearing witness with our spirit that we are children of God, [17]and if children, then heirs, heirs of God and fellow heirs with Christ, provided we suffer with him in order that we may also be glorified with him. (Rom 8:16-17)

The baptized can maintain both the confidence of being God's children and the realization that they will be conformed to Jesus Christ in suffering before they inherit glory. Sharing in Christ's death and resurrection is a lifelong process that begins in Baptism.

DISCUSS

1. How did St. Paul's experience of Christ on the road to Damascus, his blindness, and his baptism help him to understand the relationship that exists between Jesus Christ and his Church?

2. Discuss your baptism and similarities between your entrance into the Church and St. Paul's.

3. Reflecting on St. Paul's teaching of the unity of Christ with all the baptized, how might you live your life "in Christ," rather than living for your own selfish pursuits.

4. During the Baptism ritual, after a person is baptized, he or she is clothed in a white garment. In light of St. Paul's teaching on Baptism, what new insights have you gained into this symbol?

5. How do you see Christ's command to spread the Gospel to the ends of the world being lived out by the early Church? by the present-day Church? by you?

PRACTICE

Make a conscious effort this week to foster your relationship with Christ and his Church.

Session 2

TO BE FORGIVEN

St. Paul on Baptism and Reconciliation

CONSIDER

When St. Paul wrote his Letter to the Romans, he had not yet visited the city but had met some individual members, who are listed in a long series of greetings in chapter 16. This letter is Paul's personal introduction to a community he hoped to visit after his Pentecost pilgrimage to Jerusalem in the spring of A.D. 58. The epistle to the Romans treats many important issues, including some of the topics covered in Galatians on faith, righteousness, and the Torah ("the law").

Romans 6:1-2 begins with rhetorical questions that build upon St. Paul's earlier treatment of the greater power of grace to overcome sin. Though Adam's sin affected the whole human race by introducing death to everyone, Christ's redemption was more powerful in overcoming sin and death (Rom 5:12-21). He then poses rhetorical questions that could be asked by someone who argued through *reductio ad absurdum*: Are we to continue sinning more in order to make grace abound still more? Instead of answering rhetorically, Paul advances the argument with a discussion of the way Christians have died to sin and cannot continue in it.

The next stage of the argument introduces Baptism as the means by which Christians die to sin:

> ³Do you not know that all of us who have been baptized into Christ Jesus were baptized into his death? ⁴We were buried therefore with him by baptism into death, so that as Christ was raised

from the dead by the glory of the Father, we too might walk in newness of life.

⁵For if we have been united with him in a death like his, we shall certainly be united with him in a resurrection like his. ⁶We know that our old self was crucified with him so that the sinful body might be destroyed, and we might no longer be enslaved to sin. ⁷For he who has died is freed from sin. ⁸But if we have died with Christ, we believe that we shall also live with him. ⁹For we know that Christ being raised from the dead will never die again; death no longer has dominion over him. (Rom 6:3-9)

Here Paul teaches strongly that Baptism is the means by which Christians die to sin. The power of Baptism derives from the way it sacramentally unites a Christian to Jesus Christ's death, burial, and resurrection. Though Paul does not explicitly connect the action of entering the water with death and exiting the water with resurrection, this has been a common interpretation of the sacramental action in light of this passage. Paul asserts a great power to Baptism in the spiritual realm: it not only gives a person union with Jesus' death, but it offers hope for the resurrection of the body in the future, a topic St. Paul develops in Romans 8.

CHOOSE YOUR WEAPONS

Romans 6:13 sets before the Christian the choice to use the members of their bodies as "weapons of wickedness" or "weapons of righteousness." Some translations (such as the RSV) use the more general term "instruments," but the Greek word *hopla* specifically refers to weapons. Furthermore, the mention of being slaves (Rom 6:16-18, 20) or being set free (Rom 6:18, 20, 22) highlights the gladiatorial image, since most gladiators were slaves. These combats, unfortunately, were designated as "games," but the outcome was either life or death. Our combat for God's righteousness against sin, impurity, and iniquity is a struggle for eternal life or death.

In 2007, Pope Benedict XVI announced that, beginning on the eve of the Solemnity of Sts. Peter and Paul, 2008, through June 29, 2009, there would be a Jubilee Year of St. Paul. This will commemorate what is regarded as the 2,000th anniversary of the saint's birth.

The Pope has called for "a series of liturgical, cultural and ecumenical events ... as well as various pastoral and social initiatives, all of them inspired by Pauline spirituality." In addition to these activities scheduled throughout the year, plans are also in the works for organized tours to the sites in Rome, Greece, and Turkey that are associated with St. Paul's life and ministry.

Naturally, special attention will be paid to pilgrimages to the apostle's tomb, located at the Basilica of St. Paul Outside the Walls in Rome. In addition to several events specifically located at and oriented toward the basilica, the Pope will inaugurate the Jubilee Year from this location by presiding at the celebration of First Vespers.

Please visit http://annopaolino.org for news, events, and services pertaining to this special Pauline celebration.

The fact of the power of the sacrament does not remove the Christian from the need to make great effort in overcoming sin throughout life. In fact, Romans 6:12-23 uses the images of gladiatorial combat in the arena to indicate the mighty struggle we make to use the members of our bodies as weapons for righteousness rather than weapons for sin. That basic choice must be made daily throughout life. However, Baptism so unites a Christian with the most basic paschal mystery of Jesus' saving death and resurrection that one can say that he or she has died to sin and already has a share in the hope for the resurrection. Indeed, so powerful is Baptism that later St. Peter will write: "Baptism . . . now saves you" (1 Pet 3:21).

Just as Jesus was raised up in glory, so will we be united with him in resurrection.

INVESTIGATE

ST. PAUL ON BAPTISM

 Look up the following passages and jot down some key concepts that St. Paul emphasized about Baptism in each.

PASSAGE	KEY CONCEPTS
Ephesians 4:1-13	
Colossians 2:8-15	
Titus 3:4-7	

STUDY

On Easter Sunday, Christ our Lord commissioned the apostles to hear confessions: "Receive the Holy Spirit. If you forgive the sins of any, they are forgiven; if you retain the sins of any, they are retained" (Jn 20:22-23). This power derives from the Lord's saving death and resurrection, and his authority as God enables him to pass this on to the apostles. However, the precise form of hearing confession is not specified here or elsewhere in the New Testament, except for the obvious assumption that the penitent must confess sins audibly to the one hearing the confession in order for him to know whether to retain or forgive the sin.

St. Paul does not explicitly speak about the rites of hearing confessions and offering absolution, but he certainly addresses the fact that he has authority to forgive and reconcile sinners, and that this power remains in the Church. Paul addresses this in his Second Letter to the Corinthians, which he wrote from Ephesus around A.D. 55. The community continued to experience a variety of difficulties, which Paul addresses in this letter. There are three relevant passages.

A. 2 Corinthians 2:5-11

> [5]But if any one has caused pain, he has caused it not to me, but in some measure — not to put it too severely — to you all. [6]For such a one this punishment by the majority is enough; [7]so you should rather turn to forgive and comfort him, or he may be overwhelmed by excessive sorrow. [8]So I beg you to reaffirm your love for him. [9]For this is why I wrote, that I might test you and know whether you are obedient in everything. [10]Any one whom you forgive, I also forgive. What I have forgiven, if I have forgiven anything, has been for your sake in the presence of Christ, [11]to keep Satan from gaining the advantage over us; for we are not ignorant of his designs. (2 Cor 2:5-11)

This passage contains a number of important elements of the theology of confession. The person spoken of here may be the same man who committed incest with his father's wife (1 Cor 5:1-5).

First, notice that Paul does not take the offense personally to himself. Rather, he sees the sin as affecting the whole community. This is the shadow side of his doctrine of the mystical Body of Christ. *While the gifts of the Holy Spirit are given for the common good, to build up the whole Church, the sins committed by individual members have a negative effect on the whole community.* This teaching underscores the need for the sacrament of confession of sins to take place in a Church context. The sins are not simply about individual, private actions that offend God. Sins offend God, and they harm the whole Body of Christ.

Second, the sinner has already demonstrated sorrow for his deeds. That seems so clear to Paul, who is hundreds of miles away in Ephesus, that he urges the local Corinthians to accept this sorrow and forgive. Remember that Jesus our Lord had given the apostles the option of forgiving or retaining sins, so the presumed criteria for this decision must have been linked to the sinner demonstrating true sorrow for sin.

> ### IN PERSONA CHRISTI
> "In the sacred mysteries, [the priest] does not represent himself and does not speak expressing himself, but speaks for the Other, for Christ."
> — POPE BENEDICT XVI,
> *Homily for the Chrism Mass* (April 5, 2007)

Third, Paul forgives the sinner and urges the community to do the same. He exhorts them to a love that will reconcile the sinner to the community. This love will be shown in their public and communal profession of forgiveness.

Fourth, Paul states that he forgives literally in the *face* of Christ. This expression may simply indicate that Paul is in Christ's presence. However, "face" also can refer to "personhood." This phrase means that St. Paul claims to act *in persona Christi*, which is precisely the way St. Jerome translated it in the Latin Vulgate. The authority exercised in the Sacrament of Penance and Reconciliation is not the merely personal forgiveness of the priest or of any other Christian. Rather, the power that gives people the assurance of the forgiveness of sins is that the priest or bishop acts in the "person of Christ," and offers the forgiveness Jesus authorized them to give on Easter Sunday night.

B. 2 Corinthians 5:18-21

> [18]All this is from God, who through Christ reconciled us to himself and gave us the ministry of reconciliation; [19]that is, God was in Christ reconciling the world to himself, not counting their trespasses against them, and entrusting to us the message of reconciliation. [20]So we are ambassadors for Christ, God making his appeal through us. We beseech you on behalf of Christ, be reconciled to God. [21]For our sake he made him to be sin who knew no sin, so that in him we might become the righteousness of God. (2 Cor 5:18-21)

First, notice that Paul speaks of reconciliation as a service or ministry (*diakonia* in Greek). He closely connects the ideas of God's two actions: God reconciles the world through Christ and gives the ministry of reconciliation. The Greek grammar indicates that the link between these actions is quite intentionally strong.

Second, the link is clarified by Paul's claim to be an ambassador of Christ through whom God makes his appeal of reconciliation. Ambassadors are trusted representatives of a king or government. The ambassador is backed up by the authority of the one who sent him, so long as he is faithful to the king's message and mission. In this case, Paul has true authority to reconcile sinners to God through Jesus Christ. This is another way of speaking about his ability to act *in persona Christi*.

Third, St. Paul explains the power behind his authority by describing one aspect of the redemption. Jesus Christ is the one who knew no sin; how can he be the one that God made into sin? This text is explained by the fact that Israelite sacrifices had a variety of categories, including the sin offering. The Hebrew word for this type of sacrifice is simply one word, derived from the Hebrew word "sin" (Lev 4:14 and dozens of other verses). Jesus was made to be a sin offering — that is, his death on the cross is a sacrifice for the sins of the world. Therefore, the reconciliation that the priest offers in the confessional is a way to encounter Christ's saving sacrifice on the cross, much like baptism into his death enables the Christian to rise with him (Rom 6:1-6). In this context, consider that the connection with Christ's resurrection also exists for confession, since on Easter Sunday Christ told his disciples of their ambassadorial authority to forgive or retain sins (Jn 20:23).

Fourth, the power of Christ's reconciliation, which is communicated by his ambassadors, is not a mere juridical declaration of innocence. Rather, the goal is for the Christian to "become the righteousness of God" (v. 21). This indicates that, truly, grace is given in the Sacrament of Penance, a grace which makes for a true transformation of the penitent into God's righteousness. Remember, in 1 Corinthians 1:30, St. Paul identifies Jesus Christ as the righteousness of God. This connection indicates that the Christian becomes transformed into the righteousness of God that Jesus Christ personifies. The grace of the sacraments changes us into other Christs.

C. 2 Corinthians 7:8-11

> [8]For even if I made you sorry with my letter, I do not regret it [now] (though I did regret it [then]), for I see that that letter grieved you, though only for a while. [9]As it is, I rejoice, not because you were grieved, but because you were grieved into repenting; for you felt a godly grief, so that you suffered no loss through us.
> [10]For godly grief produces a repentance that leads to salvation and brings no regret, but worldly grief produces death. [11]For see what earnestness this godly grief has produced in you, what eagerness to clear yourselves, what indignation, what alarm, what longing, what zeal, what punishment! At every point you have proved yourselves guiltless in the matter. (2 Cor 7:8-11)

This text refers to another letter Paul sent to the Corinthians, in addition to the two available in the Bible. No copy of that letter exists. The issue at stake in this passage is true guilt versus false guilt. St. Paul recognizes that his previous letter caused the

Corinthians to feel guilt and sorrow. Paul takes a pastoral approach and uses their sorrow to explain two kinds of sorrow: salvific and deadly. This is particularly important in the modern world, where feelings of guilt are shunned and rejected as one of the most dangerous emotions a person can experience. St. Paul's insights may help us sort through the issue of authentic sorrow for sin.

What constitutes the difference between true and false guilt? One element is the purpose the sorrow serves:

- Is the sorrow merely an opportunity for the guilty person to express himself or herself?

- Does it let out an emotion of ill ease over certain behaviors that may have offended other persons or may compromise someone's high opinion of himself? For instance, "I am of such a high quality of person that I am simply mortified and embarrassed that I have acted like people of a lower type than I."

Such guilt does not raise a person beyond his own limits; it tends to keep the person trapped within the ego. It may feed pride or it may become a self-destructive emotional guilt that controls and eventually destroys someone's life. Because such emotionalized guilt is destructive, modern pop psychology and moralizing advise the present culture against allowing people to accept any guilt in their lives. In fact, the Sacrament of Penance is denigrated as an institution that cripples people emotionally by causing more guilt — that is, "Catholic guilt" — in everyday life.

On the contrary, St. Paul commends a sorrow that is in accord with God. This means that guilt is recognized for having broken moral principles and for contradicting God's law. Such sorrow is possible only for someone who accepts mature responsibility for his or her actions, without blaming others and without denying the seriousness of the deeds. When such sorrow is brought before God, it leads to conversion, the "metanoia" — that is, a turning around from a wrong path headed to sin and destruction by turning toward God, who directs the person to salvation and righteous, holy behavior.

This type of saving sorrow and guilt needs to be encouraged among those who are in fact guilty of breaking God's law. Even though we may seem judgmental, in fact we are simply accepting as fact that God and his Church identify some behaviors as sin and evil. The advantage for a Christian recognition of this comes from the confidence we can have that Jesus Christ will encounter the guilty sinner in the confessional and offer forgiveness and true reconciliation with God. Christ will use the priests who hear the confessions as his ambassadors who can legitimately announce God's message of reconciliation and peace.

Of course, the authority of a priest to be an ambassador of Christ who can officially extend reconciliation to other Christians in the Sacrament of Penance does not preclude the need for all Christians to forgive one another the wrongs that are done. Paul exhorts this mutual forgiveness in Colossians 3:12-15:

> [12]Put on then, as God's chosen ones, holy and beloved, compassion, kindness, lowliness, meekness, and patience, [13]forbearing one another and, if one has a complaint against another, forgiving each other; as the Lord has forgiven you, so you also must forgive. [14]And above all these put on love, which binds everything together in perfect harmony. [15]And let the peace of Christ rule in your hearts, to which indeed you were called in the one body. And be thankful. (Col 3:12-15)

The Sacrament of Penance and Reconciliation is a distinctive gift from God. However, St. Paul teaches here what Jesus Christ had taught in the Lord's Prayer: "Forgive us our trespasses as we forgive those who trespass against us" (see Mt 6:12). The nuance that Paul makes here is that, based on the forgiveness we have already received from the Lord, we ought to forgive others (v. 13). The gift of God's forgiveness can spread out to others and act as a powerful force within the Church, along with love, patience, and other virtues.

DISCUSS

1. How have you used the members of your body as weapons of righteousness? What did you need to fight against in those struggles? How have you used the members of your body as weapons of sin? Against what did you struggle then?

2. Colossians 2:8-15 presents some of the manifold powers of Baptism. What are they, and why is it important for St. Paul to link them to Christ's divinity?

3. In Titus 3:4-7, as elsewhere in St. Paul's writings, the apostle clearly teaches that we are justified by grace. Why is it still necessary for humans to respond to that grace, and what should that response be?

4. Reflect on the ways that sins affect the individual sinner. How do the sins of individuals affect the rest of the Church?

5. If someone asks you why Catholics confess to a priest instead of confessing directly to God, how would you explain the Sacrament of Penance to them, using Scripture alone?

PRACTICE

Make a good examination of your conscience.

Make a conscious effort this week to celebrate the Sacrament of Penance and Reconciliation.

Session 3

TO BE SEALED WITH THE HOLY SPIRIT

St. Paul on Confirmation

CONSIDER

The term "Confirmation" is not used for a sacrament in the Acts of the Apostles, but the reality is made distinct from Baptism in a number of places. The clearest example occurs in Acts 8:5-13, when the deacon Philip went to Samaria to preach and baptize. When the apostles heard of his success, they sent Peter and John to pray and lay hands on the Samaritans so that they might receive the Holy Spirit, who had not come upon them since they were only baptized in the name of Jesus (Acts 8:14-17).

Another example appears in Acts 19:1-7, when St. Paul met twelve men in Ephesus who had been baptized by John the Baptist. After his explanation of Christian Baptism, Paul baptized them. Then he laid hands upon them to receive the Holy Spirit. This episode indicates that Paul was as aware as the other apostles that Baptism is distinct from that laying on of hands to receive the Holy Spirit (i.e., Confirmation).

St. Paul's epistles do not contain explicit mention of the laying on of hands to bestow the Holy Spirit. Instead, he speaks frequently of two issues related to the reality of the Holy Spirit in Christian life: being sealed with the Holy Spirit and the role and activity of the Holy Spirit. Let us examine each one in turn.

Sealed in the Holy Spirit

St. Paul and other New Testament writers (for example, Rev 7:2-4) use a "seal" as an image for God's activity in the Christian soul:

God marks human beings as his own; they belong to him and bear the image he has stamped into them. In St. Paul's letters, this is a way to describe the influence of the Holy Spirit.

Another aspect of the image of being sealed is seen in St. Paul's use of the term to describe circumcision: "He [Abraham] received circumcision as a sign or seal of the righteousness which he had by faith . . ." (Rom 4:11). Circumcision was the sign of the covenant between God and Abraham (Gen 17:10). On the one hand, this is a permanent sign, and therefore Paul can see it as a "seal." On the other hand, it is a private sign, not on display to others, even though the whole community of Israel shares this same personal seal. These aspects apply to the seal of the Holy Spirit in Confirmation. The seal of the Spirit within the human heart is eternal and permanent: the Church identifies this as an "indelible" seal in the heart. On the other hand, it is truly personal and interior, a change in the very soul of the recipient. Yet it is also communal, in the sense that everyone who receives this sacramental seal has this gift of the Holy Spirit.

Seals were part of ancient life. Stones or pieces of metal were shaped with writing or symbols to be stamped in wax, clay, or lead in order to identify an object as belonging to a particular individual. The use of seals continues into modern times as well.

The first of St. Paul's passages about being sealed with the Holy Spirit is 2 Corinthians 1:19-22, in the context of the apostle's explanation of his delay in coming to visit the Corinthians. He wants them to know that he was not vacillating in his decision to see them, since it is contrary to Christ's person to vacillate:

> [19]For the Son of God, Jesus Christ, whom we preached among you, Silvanus and Timothy and I, was not Yes and No; but in him it is always Yes. [20]For all the promises of God find their Yes in him.

That is why we utter the Amen through him, to the glory of God. [21]But it is God who establishes us with you in Christ, and has commissioned us; [22]he has put his seal upon us and given us his Spirit in our hearts as a guarantee. (2 Cor 1:19-22)

Paul's argument proceeds from asserting Christ's fidelity, and then proclaiming that God confirms ("establishes") Christians in the same faithful Christ by giving the Holy Spirit. This passage is particularly interesting because it claims that God confirms Christians into Christ. This means that Confirmation is primarily an action of grace. Further, this Confirmation is identified with being sealed in our hearts with the Holy Spirit. Just as an ancient seal made a permanent impression into a piece of clay or lead, so does God seal our hearts with the Holy Spirit. Then St. Paul calls this a "guarantee," with the Greek term meaning something like collateral or a down payment. This presence of the Holy Spirit is God's guarantee, or surety, to strengthen the Christian and complete the process of Christian initiation already begun in Baptism.

INVESTIGATE

THE DIVINE SEAL

 Look up the following passages found in the Letter to the Ephesians about being sealed with the Holy Spirit.

PASSAGE	SEAL OF THE SPIRIT
Ephesians 1:13-14	*The guarantee of:*
Ephesians 4:30	*For:*

Ephesians 1:13-14 describes the process of the Christian convert who hears the Gospel of truth and believes in it. The next step is to be sealed with the Holy Spirit, which had been promised. This certainly refers to Christ's promise of the Holy Spirit (Acts 1:4-5), as well as the prophet Joel's prediction of the gift of the Holy Spirit (Joel 2:28-32). Just as in 2 Corinthians 1:22, the Holy Spirit is the guarantee, a sort of down payment or security that Christians will inherit eternal life with God. The reason the Holy Spirit is the guarantee is to show that only the presence of God himself can be the surety that we will inherit a heavenly dwelling with God for all eternity.

The second mention of being sealed with the Holy Spirit occurs in a section of moral exhortation. One of the reasons Christians must avoid various kinds of sin is to avoid grieving the Holy Spirit (Eph 4:30). Again, the seal of the Holy Spirit marks a Christian as being set for redemption. To commit sin is to act contrary to the impression God has made within the human heart, an impression marking off that person as set for eternal life.

INVESTIGATE

EXAMINATION OF CONSCIENCE

Ephesians 4:17-5:20 contains a well-developed examination of conscience, wherein St. Paul lists sins and faults that run contrary to the impression of the seal of the Holy Spirit (Eph 4:30). List these moral faults and discuss why they run contrary to the Holy Spirit's impression in our souls. Which of these faults are the most relevant to the modern era? Why?

The last of Paul's writings to mention being sealed is simply an affirmation of his earlier teaching: "But God's firm foundation stands, bearing this seal: 'The Lord knows those who are his,' and, 'Let every one who names the name of the Lord depart from iniquity' " (2 Tim 2:19). Two elements are highlighted in this verse. First, being sealed is the Lord's way of recognizing those who belong to him. Second, the fact of being sealed is a motivation to act like someone who has received an impression from God's seal. Live as if one is made in the image and likeness of God and avoid all forms of sin and wickedness. The seal is both a statement of the new reality of God's activity in the soul as well as a motivation to act in accord with God's gift.

STUDY

The presence of the Holy Spirit is made known in more visible ways through the gifts he bestows on Christians. St. Paul wrote three lists of these gifts, two of which list them in the context of what he taught about Baptism: 1 Corinthians 12:4-11 and Ephesians 4:7-14. This connection between Baptism and the gifts of the Holy Spirit is quite appropriate, since both Confirmation and Baptism are sacraments of Christian initiation. Both confer indelible characters or seals, so it is natural for St. Paul to discuss them together. The third list of gifts — Romans 12:3-8 — connects them with the differing roles within the one Body of Christ, as do the other two lists. However, there is no explicit mention of the Holy Spirit as the author of these gifts.

We examined 1 Corinthians 12:12-13 when discussing Baptism into the one Body of Christ, where Christ is the Head of that body (see Session 1). The section that precedes that teaching introduces the issue of the oneness within the Church and its diversity among members:

⁴Now there are varieties of gifts, but the same Spirit; ⁵and there are varieties of service, but the same Lord; ⁶and there are varieties of working, but it is the same God who inspires them all in every one. ⁷To each is given the manifestation of the Spirit for the common good. ⁸To one is given through the Spirit the utterance of wisdom, and to another the utterance of knowledge according to the same Spirit, ⁹to another faith by the same Spirit, to another gifts of healing by the one Spirit, ¹⁰to another the working of miracles, to another prophecy, to another the ability to distinguish between spirits, to another various kinds of tongues, to another the interpretation of tongues. ¹¹All these are inspired by one and the same Spirit, who apportions to each one individually as he wills. (1 Cor 12:4-11)

First, note that unity proceeds from God: the diversity of gifts comes from the same Holy Spirit; the diversity of service comes from the one Lord Jesus; and the diversity of working comes from the one God the Father. Verses 4-6 present a Trinitarian formula that emphasizes unity in God as the source of unity within the Church. At the same time, the distinction of the three divine Persons — Spirit, Lord, God — also prepare the way for the distinctiveness of gifts and activities among Christians.

Next, St. Paul emphasizes that the manifestation of the Holy Spirit is given to each Christian. The subsequent list of gifts links each gift to the Person of the Holy Spirit. This recognizes diversity already present within the Corinthian community, a diversity which existed among the Christians in the Acts of the Apostles. At the same time, it is a summons to contemporary Christians to be willing to accept the gifts that the Holy Spirit is offering each individual in the present time. This is also a call to accept the fact that other people have different gifts. This text reminds Christians to accept the diversity without either envy or disrespect, because this diversity has its origin in God the Holy Spirit. Living out the Sacrament of Confirmation will require openness to the

Holy Spirit's gifts and actively seeking them in prayer, patience, and humility.

The second list of gifts also appears in a text that speaks of Baptism and the call to unity in the Church (Eph 4:1-6 — see Session 1). However, note that the diversity of gifts is not explicitly linked to the Holy Spirit but to Christ and his ascension into heaven:

> 7But grace was given to each of us according to the measure of Christ's gift. 8Therefore it is said,
>> "When he ascended on high he led a host of captives,
>> and he gave gifts to men."
> 9(In saying, "He ascended," what does it mean but that he had also descended into the lower parts of the earth? 10He who descended is he who also ascended far above all the heavens, that he might fill all things.) 11And his gifts were that some should be apostles, some prophets, some evangelists, some pastors and teachers, 12for the equipment of the saints, for the work of ministry, for building up the body of Christ, 13until we all attain to the unity of the faith and of the knowledge of the Son of God, to mature manhood, to the measure of the stature of the fullness of Christ; 14so that we may no longer be children, tossed to and fro and carried about with every wind of doctrine, by the cunning of men, by their craftiness in deceitful wiles. (Eph 4:7-14)

As in 1 Corinthians 12, this text says that each Christian receives grace and Christ's gift. Verses 8-10 immediately link the giving of these gifts to Christ's ascension. This connection fits well with the tradition of the Acts of the Apostles, where Christ promises the gift of the Holy Spirit on the day of his ascension, and then ten days later the Holy Spirit falls upon the Blessed Virgin Mary, the apostles, and the disciples in the Upper Room, bestowing gifts of speaking in tongues, prophesying, evangelizing, teaching, and being apostles. These are precisely the gifts listed here in verse 11.

The rest of the passage continues one long sentence that describes the purpose for the diversity of gifts. They equip Christians for ministry; without these gifts, Christians may flounder on their own strength. The gifts also serve to build up the Body of Christ, the Church. No Christian receives these gifts to augment personal ambition or ego. They are oriented toward service in strengthening the bonds of unity in the Church. This unity is no mere warm feeling. Rather, it is the unity of faith: Christians are to believe all that Christ has revealed. The unity entails a spiritual maturity measured by "the fullness of Christ." Jesus' spiritual maturity is the norm for each Christian to seek. The spiritual gifts are all oriented toward this unity and Christ-like maturity. In this way, the active gifts serve the interior virtues.

 Pope Benedict, in calling the Jubilee Year of St. Paul, noted that one of the goals for the year is "unity."

The third list of gifts does not mention the Holy Spirit explicitly. However, it does return to the themes of diversity of gifts and unity in the Church. The Body of Christ is one, but the individual members each have different functions. The emphasis here is on the requirement for the individual Christian to be responsibly and actively engaged in exercising the gifts he has received:

> ³For by the grace given to me I bid every one among you not to think of himself more highly than he ought to think, but to think with sober judgment, each according to the measure of faith which God has assigned him. ⁴For as in one body we have many members, and all the members do not have the same function, ⁵so we, though many, are one body in Christ, and individually members one of another. ⁶Having gifts that differ according to the grace given to us, let us use them: if prophecy, in proportion to our faith; ⁷if service, in our serving; he who teaches, in his teaching; ⁸he who exhorts, in his exhortation; he who contributes, in liberality; he who gives aid, with zeal; he who does acts of mercy, with cheerfulness. (Rom 12:3-8)

One last point about these three lists of spiritual gifts. Not one of the lists is exactly the same as the others; in fact, each list contains gifts that the other lists do not. As a result, Christians need not see these lists as exhaustive. The Holy Spirit offers a tremendous variety of spiritual gifts, and these continue to develop through the centuries. In fact, we speak of the different religious orders in the Catholic Church as each having its own charism, from the Greek word for "gift." The task for the confirmed Christian is to expect the Holy Spirit to bestow gifts, plus the grace to act on them. As Romans 12 indicates, the responsibility to exercise the gifts of the Holy Spirit is great; it is not some frivolous luxury for those who might feel inclined to use them. The Christian needs to respond generously and willingly by freely giving these gifts away to others, for the sake of others' needs, and for the greater glory of God.

St. Paul in his Letter to the Galatians directly links the Holy Spirit with interior virtues:

> [22]But the fruit of the Spirit is love, joy, peace, patience, kindness, goodness, faithfulness, [23]gentleness, self-control; against such there is no law. [24]And those who belong to Christ Jesus have crucified the flesh with its passions and desires.
>
> [25]If we live by the Spirit, let us also walk by the Spirit. [26]Let us have no self-conceit, no provoking of one another, no envy of one another. (Gal 5:22-26)

In this passage, St. Paul speaks of the "fruit" of the Holy Spirit. The choice of "fruit" points to a profound difference from the spiritual gifts. A gift is bestowed upon a person, either in its entirety or in parts and sections. A fruit grows slowly and develops its sweetness over a length of time. This is an apt image for the Spirit's fruit of love, joy, peace, patience, kindness, goodness, faithfulness, gentleness, and self-control (or chastity). Like a fruit, each one of these virtues may begin as a blossom that smells sweet and appears beautiful. Many converts see an initial improvement in their personality, accompanied by great joy. However, blossoms fade and fall away, leaving a small, green, bitter nub. At some point, Christians find it difficult, even bitter, to try to live the virtues. Only with much time and growth does the fruit grow in size and eventually gain color. Yet even when color appears, the fruit may be hard and sour on the inside. Only full development allows the sweetness to come through. The Christian must remain united with the Church, the Body of Christ, like fruit on a tree. The sap of the Holy Spirit will continue to flow into the soul, increasing the size, color, and sweetness of the virtues.

DISCUSS

1. What did the bishop say to you when you were confirmed and he anointed your forehead with sacred chrism? How does knowing what St. Paul said about this give you a greater understanding of the meaning of those words?

2. What gifts has God given to you for the greater good of the Church? If you are in a group in which everyone knows everyone else well, tell each other what gifts you recognize in each other.

3. What enables people with diverse gifts to act as a unified body? What can we do to be more unified?

4. What is the difference between "gifts" and "fruits"?

PRACTICE

Find concrete ways to use the gifts that God has given to you for the greater good of the Church.

Session 4

THE BREAKING OF THE BREAD

St. Paul on the Eucharist

CONSIDER

Only one of St. Paul's epistles contains teaching on the Eucharist: 1 Corinthians. It contains two passages that offer two distinct perspectives on the Mass.

The earliest written occurrence of the phrase "break bread" is in 1 Corinthians 10:16-17, which is part of a discussion against having anything to do with idols:

> [16]The cup of blessing which we bless, is it not a participation [communion — *koinonia*] in the blood of Christ? The bread which we break, is it not a participation in the body of Christ? [17]Because there is one bread, we who are many are one body, for we all partake of the one bread. (1 Cor 10:16-17)

These verses clearly refer to the Mass, as seen in the other uses of the phrase. 1 Corinthians 11:24 includes in its description of the institution that, *giving thanks (eucharistesas)*, Jesus *broke the bread* he had taken up, as Mark 14:22, Matthew 26:26, and Luke 22:19 also do. These passages show that the origins of the idea are in the words of Jesus Christ. Furthermore, because Jesus himself "broke bread" in the four institution narratives, this phrase became Luke's designation for the Eucharist. In Luke 24:30-31, the two disciples at Emmaus recognized Jesus in the breaking of the bread, indicating that the essence of the Mass is the recognition of the presence of Jesus Christ in the consecration of the bread and wine. This forms the background for Acts 2:42, 46, where the early Church was "devoted . . . to the apostles' teaching and fellowship [*koinonia*, the word translated as "communion" in 1 Cor 10:16], to the breaking of bread and the prayers." St. Luke also indicates the importance of the apostles' teaching in the celebration of the Eucharist, which is continued by reading their epistles and Gospels at every Mass; their teaching about Jesus Christ nourishes our souls along with the breaking of the bread.

INVESTIGATE

CELEBRATING THE EUCHARIST

The Acts of the Apostles gives us several glimpses of St. Paul, and of the other apostles as well, celebrating the "breaking of the bread." Look up the following passages and note what each episode mentions with regard to the celebration of the Eucharist.

PASSAGE	NOTES
Acts 2:41-47	
Acts 20:7-11	
Acts 27:34-36	

STUDY

Having shown that "breaking the bread" is a Eucharistic term, we return to 1 Corinthians 10:16-17. The context of the passage shows that Paul's message concerns the importance of avoiding worship of idols (1 Cor 10:14) because the pagans are offering sacrifice to demons, and to eat the food from these sacrifices makes people participants or "communicants" with demons (1 Cor 10:19-21). This parallels the Israelites who are "communicants" in the sacrifices at the Temple (1 Cor 10:18).

The key point for Christians is that they share a kind of communion that is far more salvific than the pagan communion with demons and more intimate than the communion of Israelites with the animal sacrifices in the Temple.

The second text where St. Paul teaches about the Eucharist is 1 Corinthians 11:23-30. Not only is this the earliest written form of Jesus' institution of the Eucharist at the Last Supper, but it also includes both theological reflection and moral issues regarding the way people receive Holy Communion.

A key to St. Paul's theological reflection on the Eucharist is to see it as a sacrifice. The evidence for this idea comes from the very words of the institution of the Eucharist in 1 Corinthians 11:23-25:

> [23]For I received from the Lord what I also delivered to you, that the Lord Jesus on the night when he was betrayed took bread, [24]and when he had given thanks, he broke it, and said, "This is my body which is for you. Do this in remembrance of me." [25]In the same way also the cup, after supper, saying, "This cup is the new covenant in my blood. Do this, as often as you drink it, in remembrance of me." (1 Cor 11:23-25)

The words of the institution reveal its sacrificial nature in the mention of Jesus' blood for a new covenant. The Old Testament background for this concept lies in Exodus 24:5-8: when Moses had placed half of the blood of oxen in bowls and had splashed the other half on the altar, he proclaimed, "Behold the blood of the covenant" (Ex 24:8). In the institution of the Eucharist, Christ proclaims that the cup is his blood of the new covenant. Not only does this connect with Exodus 24, but it also is a fulfillment of the promise of a new covenant in Jeremiah 31:31-33. It is of key importance to note that the old covenant began with the sacrifice of oxen, while the new covenant is in the sacrifice of Christ's blood.

A second element from the words of institution points to the sacrificial nature of the Mass — namely, our Lord's command to "do" this. In the Old Testament, the word "do" or "make" has a wide range of meanings, one of which is *to offer sacrifice*. The English translation does not indicate this usage of "do," but it is well known throughout the Old Testament. This meaning of "do" as *sacrifice* adds weight to the other sacrificial terms in the institution of the Eucharist.

INVESTIGATE

"DOING" SACRIFICE

 The following passages use the verb "do" to mean "offering sacrifice." Look up the texts to see the variety of types of sacrifice the people of Israel were told to "do." If you are studying this as a group, divide the passages up, and after a few moments have all members report what they have discovered to the group.

PASSAGE	SACRIFICE TO "DO"
Exodus 10:25	
Leviticus 14:19, 30	
Leviticus 15:15, 30	
Leviticus 16:9, 24	
Leviticus 17:8-9	

Numbers 6:11, 17	
Numbers 15:3, 14	
Judges 13:16	
1 Kings 8:64	
2 Kings 5:17	
Jeremiah 33:18	
Ezekiel 43:25	
Ezekiel 45:17	
Ezekiel 46:1-15	

STUDY

The third point of the institution narrative suggesting sacrifice is "doing it" as a memorial of Jesus. Some want to understand the memorial as a merely human calling-to-mind of the last Passover meal our Lord celebrated. This perspective grasps neither the Old Testament understanding of memory nor the importance of memorial terminology in association with sacrifices. Modern commentators accept that remembering included some sense of making present the object of the memory. For this reason, Amos 6:10

warns, "Hush, do not remember [*hazkir*] Yahweh by name," while Psalm 20:7 proclaims, "But we in the name of Yahweh our God will cause remembrance [*nazkir*]" (author's translation). This understanding of memory as *making present* helps us understand the real presence of the Lord Jesus in the sacrament.

The sacrificial aspect of remembering appears in the Old Testament use of memorial terms for sacrifices. Four of the occurrences of "memorial" refer to the sweet-smelling smoke of incense offered with a sacrifice of meal and oil (Lev 2:2, 16; 6:15; 24:7). In other words, "memorial" refers to one specific type of Old Testament sacrifice. By using this term in his command for the disciples to "do this," Jesus is linking his action at the Last Supper with the Old Testament sacrifices and at the same time fulfilling them for the New Testament.

INVESTIGATE

EUCHARISTIC NARRATIVES

 Examine the other three New Testament narratives of the institution of the Eucharist to consider how this same evidence for the sacrificial qualities of the Eucharist appears in them.

PASSAGE	NOTES
Matthew 26:26-28	
Mark 14:22-24	
Luke 22:19-20	

Immediately after describing the institution of the Eucharist, St. Paul proceeds to clarify its sacrificial character by connecting its theological interpretation to Christ's sacrificial death on Calvary: "For as often as you eat this bread and drink the cup, you proclaim the Lord's death until he comes" (1 Cor 11:26). The meaning of the Mass is the proclamation of the death of Jesus until the time he returns at the end of the world. Since his death is the essential action of his self-sacrifice, then it follows that the Eucharist is the re-presentation of his sacrifice. This further clarifies St. Paul's teaching in 1 Corinthians 10:16-21 that sets the Eucharist in contrast to pagan and Jewish sacrifices: the sacrifice on the cross replaces those other sacrifices completely, and the Eucharist, which continues Christ's redemptive sacrifice, replaces the meals that resulted from either the pagan or the Jewish sacrifices.

A moral aspect of the interpretation of the Eucharist appears in 1 Corinthians 11:27-30:

> [27]Whoever, therefore, eats the bread or drinks the cup of the Lord in an unworthy manner will be guilty of profaning the body and blood of the Lord. [28]Let a man examine himself, and so eat of the bread and drink of the cup. [29]For any one who eats and drinks without discerning the body eats and drinks judgment upon himself. [30]That is why many of you are weak and ill, and some have died. (1 Cor 11:27-30)

First, note that this passage repeats Paul's belief in the real presence of Christ's Body and Blood in the Eucharist (1 Cor 10:16). Second, Paul implies that the Eucharist has tremendous power flowing from this real presence, since eating and drinking the Body and Blood of Christ improperly can lead to sickness and even death. A Christian is required to discern the real presence of the Body and Blood of Jesus Christ, his acceptable sacrifice made on the cross, in order to be free of guilt. This is a negative side to our Lord's teaching in John 6:54: "He who eats my flesh and drinks

my blood has eternal life, and I will raise him up at the last day."
Yet we should remember that some of his own disciples, including
Judas, could not accept his teaching that he would give them his
flesh to eat and his blood to drink: "Therefore many of his disciples said, 'This is a hard saying; who can listen to it?' " (Jn 6:60).
"After this many of his disciples drew back and no longer went
about with him" (Jn 6:66; see also Jn 6:70-71, which is the first
mention of Judas as a betrayer). Both in our Lord's and in Paul's
teaching, the Eucharist is a decisive doctrine determining one's
whole relationship with Christ and his Church.

DISCUSS

1. Why is it so important to establish the meaning of the phrase
"breaking of the bread" from other passages in the New Testament?
What other meaning might have been developed if it were considered apart from these significations in the New Testament?

2. In 1 Corinthians 10:16-21, St. Paul contrasts the Eucharist
both with pagan and with Jewish sacrifices. What relevance does
this have to Paul's understanding of the nature of the Eucharist?

3. Summarize the evidence from 1 Corinthians 11 that indicates the Eucharist is a sacrifice.

4. Discuss the importance of moral examination before receiving Holy Communion, particularly in light of St. Paul's connection of moral issues in Baptism (Rom 6) and with Confirmation
(Eph 4-5).

PRACTICE

Consider what it might mean to receive the Eucharist worthily.
How can you know this, and what should you do to ensure wor-
thy reception?

Session 5

OFFERING SACRIFICE

St. Paul on Holy Orders

CONSIDER

The letters of St. Paul contain a significant number of passages dealing with the ordained ministry. This should come as no surprise, since he was instrumental in establishing new churches throughout the Mediterranean world by his preaching and by the ordaining of leaders — bishops, priests, and deacons. The Church learns so much about her hierarchical structure from these texts, as seen in writings throughout the centuries, from the Church Fathers to the documents of Vatican II and the present day.

The first issue is the question about priesthood: Did Paul understand himself to be a priest? The language of priesthood appears in a few New Testament texts: the Letter to the Hebrews refers to Jesus Christ as the one true high priest; St. Peter speaks of Christians becoming "a holy priesthood, to offer spiritual sacrifices acceptable to God through Jesus Christ" (1 Pet 2:5; see also Rev 1:6; 5:10; 20:6). Why is this explicitly priestly language missing in St. Paul's writings?

First, remember that St. Paul had been trained as a Pharisee well versed in the Law. According to Jewish law, only members of the tribe of Levi and of the family of Aaron could become priests; it was an office passed on from father to son. As such, Paul, a member of the tribe of Benjamin, could never be qualified to be a Jewish priest — a *cohen* in Hebrew. Another word for priest exists in Hebrew — *comer* — which refers only to pagan priests. This poses a linguistic problem for early Christians, whose roots in Judaism made them reluctant to employ priesthood terms. The term *cohen* could not be used for anyone born outside that particular clan; *comer*, the term for pagan priests, would be insulting at best or blasphemous at worst. For this reason, the New Testament uses the word "priest" for Levitical priests or, once, for a pagan priest of Zeus (Acts 14:13). Instead, Christians developed another vocabulary for their ministers — deacon (a term initiated by the apostles in Acts 6), presbyter, and bishop (in Greek *episkopos*, "overseer"). The latter two terms have close equivalents in the Essene writings of the Dead Sea Scrolls, from which they may have been borrowed.

DESERT DISSIDENTS

 The Essenes began as a dissident group of priests and laity in the middle of the second century B.C., separating themselves from Jerusalem and moving to the desert, near the Dead Sea. Simon, the last of the Maccabee brothers, had made himself both high priest and king of Jerusalem in 142 B.C., which the Essenes saw as a corrupt usurpation of power. The Essenes remained in the desert until the Romans destroyed them in A.D. 68. However, before that destruction they managed to hide many of their manuscripts in caves. These documents were discovered by a Bedouin in 1947 and are now known as the Dead Sea Scrolls. Not only do these scrolls give strong support to the authenticity of the Old Testament, but the discovery of the Essene community's documents helps us understand the way many terms found in the New Testament were used among first-century Essenes.

Despite these linguistic issues, St. Paul does understand himself in a priestly way, and this understanding also applies to the men he ordained to be deacons, priests, and bishops:

¹⁵But on some points I have written to you very boldly by way of reminder, because of the grace given me by God ¹⁶to be a minister of Christ Jesus to the Gentiles in the priestly service of the gospel of God, so that the offering of the Gentiles may be acceptable, sanctified by the Holy Spirit. (Rom 15:15-16)

In this passage, Paul uses a verbal form "doing priestly ministry," with the Greek word for priest (*hieros*) forming a part of this verb. This understanding is augmented by saying that the purpose of his priestly acting is to make the Gentiles' offerings acceptable. Offering sacrifice is the constitutive action of a priest. This verse makes it plain that Paul understood his service in a priestly way. In addition, his priestly activity makes the Gentiles holy, which is another function of the priests: making things holy by their liturgical actions.

The roots of his insight can be found in a variety of passages where he understands the saving work of Jesus Christ's death as a sacrificial act understood through the prism of Israelite sacrifices: "For Christ, our paschal lamb, has been sacrificed. Let us, therefore, celebrate the festival, not with the old leaven, the leaven of malice and evil, but with the unleavened bread of sincerity and truth" (1 Cor 5:7b-8). Using the imagery of the Day of Atonement, Paul wrote that "God set forth [Jesus] as a propitiatory in his blood as a demonstration of his righteousness through the remission of previous sins in God's forbearance" (Rom 3:25; author's translation). The term "propitiatory" (in Greek *hilasterion*) refers to the covering of the Ark of the Covenant, which the high priest sprinkled with blood on the Day of Atonement.

Two other passages understand Christ's salvation as a sin offering, such as described in Leviticus 4:33 and elsewhere. First, "Sending his own Son in the likeness of sinful flesh and [as a sin offering], [God] condemned sin in the flesh" (Rom 8:3). Second, "For our sake he made him to be sin who knew no sin, so that in him we might become the righteousness of God" (2 Cor 5:21).

In Jewish law, the priests sacrificed the Passover lamb and the sin offerings, while only the high priest offered the sacrifice on the Day of Atonement. By portraying Jesus' death as a sacrificial act connected with Passover (1 Cor 5:7b-8), the Day of Atonement (Rom 3:25), and the sin offerings (Rom 8:3; 2 Cor 5:21), St. Paul teaches that Jesus is the priest who offers himself as a redemptive sacrifice.

By seeing himself as exercising a priestly service, St. Paul understands himself as continuing Christ's saving mystery. This is in harmony with his presentation on Christ's institution of the Eucharist in 1 Corinthians 11:24-25, where Paul passes on the tradition that Jesus twice commanded the disciples to "Do this in my remembrance." As noted in the chapter on the Eucharist, "memorial" has a strong connection with sacrifice (Lev 2:2, 16; 5:12; 6:15; 24:7; Num 5:18, 26; 10:10). This sacrificial understanding of the Eucharist, which Christ commanded his apostles to "do" (another term connected with sacrifice), helps interpret St. Paul's understanding of the priestly quality of his ministry. At the same time, St. Paul does not develop this aspect in great detail; the hints he offers will be developed in the early Church, as in St. Clement of Rome's *Epistle to the Corinthians* (written in A.D. 95), chapters 40-44; St. Hippolytus' *Apostolic Traditions*; and the *Didascalia Apostolorum*.

INVESTIGATE

THE "INCLUSIVE" CHURCH

 The Acts of the Apostles describes various stages in which the Church moved away from being a Jewish community to one that incorporated all nations. Write down how each episode made the Church more ethnically inclusive.

PASSAGE	NOTES
Acts 2:7-12	
Acts 2:38-41	
Acts 8:5-13	
Acts 8:26-39	
Acts 10:20-48	
Acts 11:19-26	
Acts 13:1-4	
Acts 15:1-31	

STUDY

Bishops and Deacons

Something that is developed in St. Paul's writings is his concern to establish churches and their leaders — the bishops, presbyters, and deacons. The Acts of the Apostles mentions Paul's leadership along this line at Lystra, Iconium, and Antioch, where he "appointed elders for them in every church" (Acts 14:23). He apparently established bishops and deacons in Philippi, as evidenced by the greeting in his epistle to the church he established in A.D. 50: "Paul and Timothy, servants of Christ Jesus, [t]o all the saints in Christ Jesus who are at Philippi, with the bishops and deacons" (Phil 1:1). When he ordained priests and bishops, he did so by the laying on of hands; and he instructed Timothy to do the same when he, in turn, needed to ordain other priests and bishops.

ORDINATION — OLD AND NEW

 The ordination of priests in the Old Testament is described in two nearly identical texts: Exodus 29, where God instructs Moses on how to ordain the priests, and Leviticus 8, where Moses fulfills all that the Lord told him to do.

What actions does Moses take in regard to the priests' hands?

_____

_____

_____

What are the different kinds of sacrifices included in the ordination ceremony?

_____

_____

_____

What is the meaning of the ceremonial washings?

_____

_____

_____

What kind of anointing is performed on the priests at their ordination?

_____

_____

_____

St. Paul does not develop a teaching about the theological meaning of the Christian ministry of bishops, priests, and deacons. However, three passages discuss the qualifications he expects in ministers. He wrote all three passages in the epistles known as the "Pastorals." They were addressed to St. Timothy and St. Titus, the men he had appointed as the bishops of Ephesus and Crete, respectively. The purpose of the instruction was to offer guidance on the kind of men whom Timothy and Titus should choose as bishops, priests, and deacons.

THE "PASTORAL" EPISTLES

A significant number of scholars believe that the three "Pastoral" epistles were not written by St. Paul, since the vocabulary is different from that in his other letters and the topic of bishops, priests, and deacons does not appear elsewhere. However, note that thirty-seven of the "unusual" terms appear elsewhere only in St. Luke's books — his Gospel and the Acts of the Apostles. Thirty-seven other words that are somewhat less common in Paul are also found in Luke's writings. Note also that only Luke is still with Paul as he is writing these letters (2 Tim 4:11). The simplest solution to the linguistic difficulties is that Luke was Paul's secretary and that he used some of his own vocabulary. This also makes it easier to explain other aspects, such as the less developed distinctions between bishops, priests, and deacons, which definitely appear in the writings of St. Clement of Rome and St. Ignatius of Antioch, two leaders of the next generation.

The first passage describes the virtues to seek and the vices to avoid in candidates for the offices of bishop and deacon:

[1]If any one aspires to the office of bishop, he desires a noble task. [2]Now a bishop must be above reproach, the husband of

one wife, temperate, sensible, dignified, hospitable, an apt teacher, ³no drunkard, not violent but gentle, not quarrelsome, and no lover of money. ⁴He must manage his own household well, keeping his children submissive and respectful in every way; ⁵for if a man does not know how to manage his own household, how can he care for God's church? ⁶He must not be a recent convert, or he may be puffed up with conceit and fall into the condemnation of the devil; ⁷moreover he must be well thought of by outsiders, or he may fall into reproach and the snare of the devil. (1 Tim 3:1-7)

THE GOOD BISHOP

 Make a list of the qualities of a good bishop, reflecting St. Paul's teaching in 1 Timothy 3:1-7.

_____

_____

_____

_____

_____

⁸Deacons likewise must be serious, not double-tongued, not addicted to much wine, not greedy for gain; ⁹they must hold the mystery of the faith with a clear conscience. ¹⁰And let them also be tested first; then if they prove themselves blameless let them serve as deacons. ¹¹The women likewise must be serious, no slanderers, but temperate, faithful in all things. ¹²Let deacons be the husband of one wife, and let them manage their children and their households well; ¹³for those who serve well as deacons gain a good standing for themselves and also great confidence in the faith which is in Christ Jesus. (1 Tim 3:8-13)

Make a list of the qualities of a good deacon, reflecting St. Paul's teaching in 1 Timothy 3:8-13.

_____

_____

_____

_____

_____

St. Paul considers the aspiration to be a bishop as the desire for a good work. Being a bishop had little benefit except a good position and much confidence in faith in Christ (v. 13).

It would not be long before the position of bishop usually became a death sentence, because their prominence during times of persecution made them prime targets for government officials. Even during Paul's lifetime, the possibility of harassment and persecution of bishops was more likely than the acquisition of personal perks. In such a circumstance, eagerness for the role of bishop was a positive attitude commended by the apostle.

St. Paul mentions the women in the context of teaching about the deacons. In fact, the deaconess Phoebe is mentioned in Romans 16:1. The early Fathers note that these deaconesses had specific roles with the female members of the Church, but, unlike the men, they were not ordained (St. Hippolytus, Apostolic Traditions 10, 12).

Verse 2 sets the theme for the whole passage, as is confirmed in verse 7, the concluding line about the bishops: the bishop must be above reproach and not fall into reproach. St. John Chrysostom (*Sermon X on First Timothy*) wrote that being "above reproach" summarizes the whole list of virtues in this passage.

The first qualification for being above reproach is that the bishop must be the husband of one woman. St. Justin Martyr (*Dialogue with Trypho*, Chapter CXLI) mentioned that Jews in the Old Testament could have multiple wives and concubines; this passage forbids bishops from such. Also, the bishop must be faithful to the one wife he has, without any extramarital affairs. Finally, as interpreted frequently in the early Church, the bishop could not remarry if he were widowed. At the very least, a high level of marital ethics was required of the bishop (as well as of the deacon).

THE CLERGY AND CELIBACY

Bishops and priests were permitted to be married in the early centuries of the Church. The Western Church began to forbid them to be married at the Synod of Elvira (A.D. 306). Leading theologians — such as St. Ambrose, St. Jerome, and St. Augustine — encouraged celibacy among clerics, which led to its adoption widely throughout the West. The Eastern Church continued to allow the ordination of married men, though those who were already ordained could not marry, nor could widower priests and bishops remarry. From the fourth century, a preference for celibate bishops arose; by the sixth century, Emperor Justinian made it a law that bishops had to be celibate. This has remained the law of the Eastern churches to this day.

The rest of this section on bishops lists the virtues he must seek — being temperate, sensible, dignified, hospitable (literally, a friend of strangers), skillful in teaching, and gentle — as well as the vices he must avoid — drinking too much wine, loving money, and being quick-tempered and contentious.

Finally, Paul describes two situations in the life of the bishop that are relevant to his promotion to this role. First, he needs the experience of having run his household well. This includes raising obedient and respectful children. If he can manage a home well, he can lead the Church. Second, he must not be a new convert, since this will turn his head and lead him to be tempted by pride and the rest of the devil's tricks.

Verse 7 returns to the theme by saying the bishop must have a good reputation and be above reproach. This shows Paul's concern for the way outsiders view the leaders of the Church. He may well be responding to the scandals caused by certain false teachers in Ephesus, as mentioned in this letter to Timothy.

Later in the letter, St. Paul addresses Timothy in a personal way about his own manner of conducting his role as bishop in Ephesus:

> [12]Let no one despise your youth, but set the believers an example in speech and conduct, in love, in faith, in purity. [13]Till I come, attend to the public reading of scripture, to preaching, to teaching. [14]Do not neglect the gift you have, which was given you by prophetic utterance when the elders laid their hands upon you. [15]Practice these duties, devote yourself to them, so that all may see your progress. [16]Take heed to yourself and to your teaching: hold to that, for by so doing you will save both yourself and your hearers. (1 Tim 4:12-16)

Here Paul urges his disciple Timothy to live the virtues of a bishop. The call to be an example to the believers in Ephesus is parallel to the requirement for the bishop to be "above reproach" in 1 Timothy 3:2, 7. Specifically, he is to be an example in word, deed, love, faith, and purity. The inclusion of purity relates Timothy's situation to the bishop's requirement to live a high level of marital and family morals.

Paul's encouragement to pay attention "to the public reading of scripture, to preaching, to teaching" is parallel to the need for bishops to be skillful in teaching. Finally, Timothy is reminded that he received these abilities as gifts from God. They were communicated by prophecy, which is also a gift of God's own word, and by the laying on of hands, the normal way of passing on the ordination of bishops, priests, and deacons. One might even see in this connection the link between *form* (the prophetic word in the ritual of ordination) and *matter* (the laying on of hands), the two elements that theologians will highlight in subsequent centuries as the necessary elements of a sacrament. The fact of having received a gift does not in any way preclude the need to further develop the gifts. Hence, Paul urges Timothy to cultivate them and make progress that is clear to everyone.

Priests (Presbyters)

The next two texts deal with the presbyters. The Greek word *presbyteros* literally means "elder." However, it is a mistake to simply equate this role with the older members of the community, as is seen by the use of this word in 1 Timothy 5:1-2 to refer to older men and women, while a parallel text in Titus 2:2-3 addresses the older members with the words *presbutas* and *presbutidas*. Neither of these two passages is addressing groups of leaders in the Church, while the references to presbyters in the following passages refer to specific leaders, such as those that were appointed throughout the churches in the Acts of the Apostles (Jerusalem — Acts 15:2, 4, 6; 21:18; Antioch — Acts 11:30; every church — Acts 14:23; Ephesus — Acts 20:17).

Jewish leaders used the same term: the elders are mentioned often in the three Synoptic Gospels (for example, Luke 7:3; 9:22; 20:1; 22:52; 22:66) and in Acts (4:5, 8, 23; 6:12; 23:14; 24:1; 25:15), as is the collective term *presbyterion* ("council of elders" — Acts 22:5), though never in John. The "Community Rule" discovered at Qumran also mentions the elders as a group just below the priests in rank (Community Rule VI). This demonstrates the importance of the term in describing leaders of the Jewish community, particularly the members of the Sanhedrin.

Two texts in the Pastoral Epistles mention the presbyters as having a specific role within the Church. The first, 1 Timothy 5:17-21, is focused on the presbyters alone, since 1 Timothy 3:1-13 had already treated the bishops and deacons:

> [17]Let the elders who rule well be considered worthy of double honor, especially those who labor in preaching and teaching; [18]for the scripture says, "You shall not muzzle an ox when it is treading out the grain," and, "The laborer deserves his wages." [19]Never admit any charge against an elder except on the evidence of two or three witnesses. [20]As for those who persist in sin, rebuke them in the presence of all, so that the rest may stand in fear. [21]In the presence of God and of Christ Jesus and of the elect angels I charge you to keep these rules without favor, doing nothing from partiality. (1 Tim 5:17-21)

This text centers on the presbyters' status within the Church. They deserve a double honor, especially if they teach the word of God. In fact, they should be paid for their service, as seen in the quotation from Deuteronomy 25:4, a text Paul uses to prove that apostles and all who proclaim the Gospel deserve to make their living for this service (see also 1 Cor 9:1-14). Interestingly, within the context of supporting this teaching through Scripture, Christ's teaching is quoted, as found in Luke 10:7 and Matthew 10:10. This adds weight to the argument that St. Luke may have been St. Paul's secretary for these letters.

The second issue regarding presbyters is the extra care regarding accusations against their behavior and character. It's not that Paul teaches they are exempt from fault, but that their public role may make them more prone to criticism. If they have sinned, they need to become a public spectacle, so as to discourage other presbyters from falling into the same sins.

A second passage about presbyters occurs in Titus, though it includes a description of the qualifications for bishops that is similar to those of 1 Timothy 3:1-7:

> ⁵This is why I left you in Crete, that you might amend what was defective, and appoint elders in every town as I directed you, ⁶if any man is blameless, the husband of one wife, and his children are believers and not open to the charge of being profligate or insubordinate. ⁷For a bishop, as God's steward, must be blameless; he must not be arrogant or quick-tempered or a drunkard or violent or greedy for gain, ⁸but hospitable, a lover of goodness, master of himself, upright, holy, and self-controlled; ⁹he must hold firm to the sure word as taught, so that he may be able to give instruction in sound doctrine and also to confute those who contradict it. (Ti 1:5-9)

Titus was placed in Crete for two reasons: to correct the problems resulting from any deficiencies in the teaching that had been given the converts there and also to appoint presbyters and bishops in each city. The reader must assume that the qualifications for the bishop also apply to the presbyter, much as was the case with the deacons in 1 Timothy 3:1-13.

The final point to be made here is that the earliest Christian writers often address the issues of the bishops, presbyters, and deacons. First came St. Clement of Rome, in A.D. 95, who wrote an epistle to the Corinthians to order them to restore the bishops, presbyters, and deacons they had kicked out of office. Particularly, chapters 40-44 describe the necessity of offering sacrifices by the high priest, priests, and Levites (ch. 40) as the parallel to the bishops, priests, and deacons offering sacrifices (chs. 42, 44). This was written barely thirty years after the death of Peter and Paul.

Second, St. Ignatius, the bishop of Antioch, who died around A.D. 107, wrote seven letters to different churches, in which he frequently raised the issue of the absolute necessity of the bishop, his presbyters, and deacons as "God's order" (*Magnesians*, ch. 6).

They are necessary for the celebration of the Eucharistic sacrifice (*Philadelphians*, ch. 4; *Smyrneans*, ch. 8) and for the existence of the Church itself (*Trallians*, ch. 3). Similarly, the *Didache* teaches the importance of bishops and deacons, who must be honored (ch. 15), so that the "sacrifice" of the "breaking of the bread" may be offered on Sunday, "the Lord's Day" (ch. 14).

Third, by the year A.D. 200, St. Hippolytus of Rome describes the procedures for ordaining bishops, presbyters, and deacons in the *Apostolic Traditions*. The prayers for ordination recognize their role in "exercising the sovereign priesthood" and offering the gifts as well as the forgiving of sins (ch. 3).

Clearly, St. Paul's teaching on the bishops, presbyters, and deacons had a major impact on the early Church. Not only were these authors early, but they came from diverse areas: Clement wrote from Rome to Corinth, using the same teaching about the sacrificial and priestly role of bishops, presbyters, and deacons. St. Ignatius came from Antioch (in Syria) and used the same teaching for five communities and one bishop (Polycarp, a twenty-year-long disciple of St. John the Apostle) in Asia Minor and one community in Macedonia (Philippi).

DISCUSS

1. What were the linguistic challenges faced by St. Paul and the early Church in speaking about a Christian priesthood? How were these problems resolved?

2. List the passages indicating that St. Paul saw Christ's redemptive work as a priestly sacrifice. How did this affect his understanding of the Christian priesthood?

3. What are the original meanings of the Greek words for bishop and priest? Do these negate or support the ways these terms are used today in the Church?

4. What are the moral ramifications of accepting the offices of bishop, priest, and deacon? Relate this to the moral demands that a Christian commits to in receiving the Sacraments of Baptism, Confirmation, and the Eucharist.

PRACTICE

What have you done to encourage young men to consider a vocation to the priesthood? What else can you do to encourage these vocations?

Session 6

TO BECOME ONE FLESH

St. Paul on Matrimony

CONSIDER

No one should be surprised that marriage formed an important element within Christian teaching. The sources of this concern reach back to Genesis 2:21-25, when the Lord God responded to the man's loneliness by making a woman who was, as the man said, "bone of my bones and flesh of my flesh" (Gen 2:23), truly his suitable partner (Gen 2:20), which made it worthwhile for a man to leave his father and mother so as to cleave to his wife (Gen 2:24). Later texts will present legislation about marriage (Ex 20:14; Deut 5:18; Lev 18; 20:10-20) and the wisdom of a good marriage (Prov 12:4; 31:10-31). Jesus taught against adultery and lust (Mt 5:27-28) and divorce (Mt 5:31-32; 19:3-9; Mk 10:2-12), and he joined the wedding celebration at Cana, the site of his first miracle (Jn 2:1-11).

In 1 Corinthians 7:1-40, St. Paul treats a variety of specific situations regarding marriage in response to questions that the Corinthians had sent him while he lived in Ephesus. It is useful to break this long passage down into component parts.

> ¹Now concerning the matters about which you wrote. It is well for a man not to touch a woman. ²But because of the temptation to immorality, each man should have his own wife and each woman her own husband. ³The husband should give to his wife her conjugal rights, and likewise the wife to her husband. ⁴For the wife does not rule over her own body, but the husband does; likewise the husband does not rule over his own body, but the wife

does. ⁵Do not refuse one another except perhaps by agreement for a season, that you may devote yourselves to prayer; but then come together again, lest Satan tempt you through lack of self-control. ⁶I say this by way of concession, not of command. (1 Cor 7:1-6)

Verse 1 counterbalances sensualists who hold that sexual gratification is a necessity in life. By exhorting men not to touch women, Paul assumes that a person can live without sex. This idea ran as contrary to the assumptions of people in his world as it does to many modern assumptions about life.

Yet in verse 2 he makes it clear that fornication is a very serious sin, such as can preclude the possibility of inheriting the kingdom of God (see 1 Cor 6:9 where the *pornoi* [or "immoral"] are the people who commit the *porneia* ["adultery"] in 1 Cor 7:2). Therefore, St. Paul proposes marriage as a remedy to uncontrolled sexual inclination. Keep in mind that control of sexual urges was not the original purpose of marriage, since the first man and woman had not yet committed the original sin and therefore did not have the disordered desires that result from the fall into sin. Rather, the purpose of the man and woman becoming one flesh (Gen 2:24) was that they might be suitable companions to each other.

Nonetheless, since the Fall, disordered sexual desires are a reality, and marriage is a proper and even holy channel for those desires. In fact, verse 3 recognizes the conjugal union

1 Corinthians 7 clearly highlights the unitive role of sexuality in Genesis 2:24. The procreative is not introduced to this narrative (which includes Gen 2-4) until after the Fall, in Genesis 3. However, the creation of the human beings in Genesis 1:26-30 highlights the procreative component, since God's command to "be fruitful and multiply" was not a math problem but rather the first commandment given in the Bible.

as a right that each spouse owes the other spouse equally. So much is this true that Paul teaches that the wife has authority over her husband's body, and that the husband has authority over his wife's body (v. 4). For this reason, husbands and wives ought not refrain from sharing these conjugal rights, except for a short amount of mutually agreed-upon time for prayer (v. 5).

> ⁷I wish that all were as I myself am. But each has his own special gift from God, one of one kind and one of another.
> ⁸To the unmarried and the widows I say that it is well for them to remain single as I do. ⁹But if they cannot exercise self-control, they should marry. For it is better to marry than to be aflame with passion. (1 Cor 7:7-9)

In verse 7, St. Paul states his personal preference that the whole Christian community be celibate, as he is. At the same time, he recognizes that each Christian has his own gift from God. This recognition of the differing gifts among Christians is consistent with Christ's teaching that being celibate for the kingdom of God is a gift for certain Christians (Mt 19:12). Still, Paul urges the unmarried and the widowed to remain celibate, so long as they are not so tempted to sexual misconduct that they would end up burning, not only with passion in this life but also into eternity — that is, in the hell Paul never mentions.

> ¹⁰To the married I give charge, not I but the Lord, that the wife should not separate from her husband ¹¹(but if she does, let her remain single or else be reconciled to her husband) — and that the husband should not divorce his wife.
> ¹²To the rest I say, not the Lord, that if any brother has a wife who is an unbeliever, and she consents to live with him, he should not divorce her. ¹³If any woman has a husband who is an unbeliever, and he consents to live with her, she should not divorce him. ¹⁴For the unbelieving husband is consecrated through his wife, and the unbelieving wife is consecrated through her husband. Otherwise, your children would be unclean, but as

it is they are holy. ¹⁵But if the unbelieving partner desires to separate, let it be so; in such a case the brother or sister is not bound. For God has called us to peace. ¹⁶Wife, how do you know whether you will save your husband? Husband, how do you know whether you will save your wife? (1 Cor 7:10-16)

Verses 10-11 begin a new section, which is no longer based on Paul's personal opinion but on the Lord's own command: wives and husbands ought not separate from their spouses. Remaining together in marriage is the teaching of the prophet Malachi: "For I hate divorce, says the LORD the God of Israel" (Mal 2:16). Jesus also prohibits divorce in his teaching (Mt 5:31-32; 19:3-9; Mk 10:2-12).

THE PAULINE PRIVILEGE

A sacramental marriage between two baptized people that has been consummated cannot be broken by anything other than death. However, 1 Corinthians 7:12-15 speaks of a situation where at least one spouse is not "a believer," meaning not baptized. If a couple enters marriage before either is baptized, they have a non-sacramental and purely natural marriage. If, after marriage, one becomes a Christian and the non-Christian spouse does not wish to be baptized and makes the marriage intolerable, then this natural marriage can be dissolved.

Then verse 12 returns to Paul's personal opinion and advice about remaining with one's spouse even if he or she is not a believer. His hope is that the believing spouse may sanctify the unbelieving spouse and their children. If the unbeliever separates from the Christian spouse, let him or her separate, since "God has called us to peace" (v. 15). However, no one can be sure whether the Christian may save the unbelieving spouse (v. 16).

¹⁷Only, let every one lead the life which the Lord has assigned to him, and in which God has called him. This is my rule in all the churches. ¹⁸Was any one at the time of his call already circum-

cised? Let him not seek to remove the marks of circumcision. Was any one at the time of his call uncircumcised? Let him not seek circumcision. [19]For neither circumcision counts for anything nor uncircumcision, but keeping the commandments of God. [20]Every one should remain in the state in which he was called. [21]Were you a slave when called? Never mind. But if you can gain your freedom, avail yourself of the opportunity. [22]For he who was called in the Lord as a slave is a freedman of the Lord. Likewise he who was free when called is a slave of Christ. [23]You were bought with a price; do not become slaves of men. [24]So, brethren, in whatever state each was called, there let him remain with God.

[25]Now concerning the unmarried, I have no command of the Lord, but I give my opinion as one who by the Lord's mercy is trustworthy. [26]I think that in view of the impending distress it is well for a person to remain as he is. [27]Are you bound to a wife? Do not seek to be free. Are you free from a wife? Do not seek marriage. [28]But if you marry, you do not sin, and if a girl marries she does not sin. Yet those who marry will have worldly troubles, and I would spare you that. [29]I mean, brethren, the appointed time has grown very short; from now on, let those who have wives live as though they had none, [30]and those who mourn as though they were not mourning, and those who rejoice as though they were not rejoicing, and those who buy as though they had no goods, [31]and those who deal with the world as though they had no dealings with it. For the form of this world is passing away. (1 Cor 7:17-31)

The next section (1 Cor 7:17-24) lays down the principle of remaining in the state in which the Christian was first called to the faith, without trying to change it. This applies to circumcision or uncircumcision, being a slave or being free, being married or single. Paul simply advises people not to change their status. His motive is found in verse 31, where he points out that "the form of this world is passing away." Implied in this idea is that the end of the world is imminent; therefore, there is no purpose in changing one's status, particularly regarding marriage. Why start a family if the present form of the world is about to disappear? As time goes on, St. Paul changes his expectation about the imminence of the end of the world and has a much more positive view of marriage. That will be developed in Ephesians 5:21-33. Here he continues to promote celibacy, without forbidding marriage. The key to understanding this is that he believes that "the appointed time has grown very short" (v. 29); therefore, long-term, future plans are not very prudent in his view.

> [32]I want you to be free from anxieties. The unmarried man is anxious about the affairs of the Lord, how to please the Lord; [33]but the married man is anxious about worldly affairs, how to please his wife, [34]and his interests are divided. And the unmarried woman or girl is anxious about the affairs of the Lord, how to be holy in body and spirit; but the married woman is anxious about worldly affairs, how to please her husband. [35]I say this for your own benefit, not to lay any restraint upon you, but to promote good order and to secure your undivided devotion to the Lord.
>
> [36]If any one thinks that he is not behaving properly toward his betrothed, if his passions are strong, and it has to be, let him do as he wishes: let them marry — it is no sin. [37]But whoever is firmly established in his heart, being under no necessity but having his desire under control, and has determined this in his heart, to keep her as his betrothed, he will do well. [38]So that he who marries his betrothed does well; and he who refrains from marriage will do better.
>
> [39]A wife is bound to her husband as long as he lives. If the husband dies, she is free to be married to whom she wishes, only in the Lord. [40]But in my judgment she is happier if she remains as she is. And I think that I have the Spirit of God. (1 Cor 7:32-40)

The only argument Paul adds to his personal view about his preference for celibacy until the end time is that the single person can focus his or her attention on the things of the Lord. This would give a person more freedom to preach, teach, learn the faith, and pray. The celibate person is freer to travel, without the concerns

The subject of St. Paul's teaching on the Second Coming of Christ so permeates his epistles that it can be the subject of an entire book. It is important to note a few of the themes he covers:

- **1 Thessalonians 4:13-5:10** addresses concerns of the early Christians about what will happen to those people who die before the imminent coming of Christ.
- **2 Thessalonians 1:5-10** places the present sufferings in perspective through the promise of revenge on the persecutors.
- **2 Thessalonians 2** teaches people not to believe those who say Christ has already come a second time.
- **1 Corinthians 15** focuses on the truth of Christ's resurrection and its connection to his future coming.
- **2 Corinthians 5** treats the nature of the body and the judgment people will undergo at the Second Coming.
- **Romans 8:18-32** centers attention on the hope for the Second Coming that saves us, with an emphasis on the effects Christ's return will have on creation and our glory.
- **Philippians 3:20-21** recognizes our heavenly citizenship and the hope of a glorified body, which makes Paul desire death (Phil 1:21-24).
- **Colossians 3:4** motivates moral behavior in this life with hope for being glorified with Christ.
- **1 Timothy 6:14-16** also encourages moral purity by hope of the Second Coming of Christ.
- **2 Timothy 4:1-2ff** encourages fidelity to the Christian mission on the basis of hope in the Second Coming.
- **Titus 2:11-14** explains the way God's grace works on the basis of its preparing us to meet Christ at his Second Coming.
- **Ephesians** does not mention the Second Coming, and it is there that his teaching on marriage points Christians to live a marital spirituality for the long term.

and restraints of a family to hold him or her back. This was Paul's experience as he traveled the Mediterranean world preaching the Gospel of Christ. He could take risks, including putting his own life in danger, without worrying about the consequences his martyrdom would have on a family. He simply suggested extending this freedom to all Christians.

Here is one last point about St. Paul's linking of a call to celibacy with the imminence of the end times. In a way, Christian chastity becomes a sign of the hope for the future. One lives without family in this life because God promises a new type of family after the resurrection of the dead. As such, celibacy is a sign of life for the final resurrection at the end of time. This is also seen in the Book of Revelation, which describes the one hundred and forty-four thousand as male virgins (Rev 14:3-4). This is a powerful sign. However, it must be balanced by St. Paul's teaching in Ephesians, where marriage is a sign of Christ's commitment to the Church, a covenantal love that will be made full only at the Last Judgment and the resurrection from the dead. Both celibacy and marriage become signs of the future hope of the world in Christ's Second Coming.

INVESTIGATE

WHAT DID JESUS TEACH ABOUT MARRIAGE?

Jesus did not offer very extensive teachings on marriage: only three texts, two of which parallel each other. He also attended a wedding, though he does not expound much on the subject of marriage there. The reason for the lack of teaching is that marriage and family were more stable among the Jews than they were in the gentile world to which Paul had been sent. The main issue of Jesus' teaching concerns a dispute between two rabbinic schools on divorce: Hillel's school allowed divorce for a matter as small as "spoiling the cooking," while Rabbi Shammai allowed divorce only for adultery (Mishnah, Tractate Gittin 9:10).

Look up the following passages relating to Jesus' teaching on marriage in the Gospels. How do they compare to what St. Paul taught?

PASSAGE	NOTES
Matthew 5:31-32	
Matthew 19:3-12	
Mark 10:2-9	
John 2:1-11	

STUDY

In Ephesians 5:18, 21-33, St. Paul presents a theology of marriage within the context of a general principle of being filled with the Holy Spirit:

> [18]Do not get drunk on wine but be filled with the Spirit. . . .
> [21]Subjecting yourselves to one another out of fear of Christ. [22]Wives, to your own husbands, as to the Lord, [23]because the man is the head of the wife as Christ is the head of the church, himself the Savior of the body. [24]But, as the church is subject to Christ, so also are wives to their husbands in everything. [25]Husbands, love your wives, as Christ loved the church and gave himself up for her, [26]so that he might make her holy, cleansing her by a washing of water through the word, [27]so that he might present to himself the church in splendor, not having a spot or wrinkle

or any such thing, that she might be holy and blameless. [28]Thus husbands ought to love their wives as their own bodies. The one who loves his own wife loves himself. [29]For no one, then, hates his own flesh, but nourishes and takes care of it, as Christ does the church, [30]because we are members of his body. [31]"On account of this a man shall leave his father and mother and be joined to his wife, and the two shall become one flesh." [32]This mystery is great, and I speak of Christ and the church. [33]Nevertheless, let each one of you love his own wife as himself, and let the wife fear the husband. (Eph 5:18, 21-33; author's translation)

First, note that the unit begins with a command not to get drunk on wine but to be filled with the Holy Spirit instead. The command to be filled with the Holy Spirit is the main verb, upon which follow the various participles in the subsequent clauses — for example, speaking to one another in hymns, singing, playing psalms, and giving thanks (Eph 5:19-20).

Then verse 21 begins a whole new section (Eph 5:21-6:9), urging Christians to be subject to one another as another aspect of being filled with the Holy Spirit. This section commends mutual submission of spouses, children and parents, and slaves and masters. Such mutual submission appears to be a rather odd component of being filled with the Holy Spirit. It is easier to associate Christian life in the Spirit with the enthusiasm of singing, hymns, and thanksgiving, but here St. Paul sees the fullness of the Spirit within the sets of relationships that were normal in the first century and later. Yet these relationships needed to be transformed and purified by mutual submission in order to go beyond their merely human dimensions.

The segment on marriage (vv. 22-33) is the focus of this discussion. It begins with a call to submit out of fear of Christ, and it ends with a call for wives to fear their husbands. Though many modern readers recoil from fear as a virtue, here the meaning of fear is not the abject terror and trembling associated with dread of evil realities. Rather, this is the fear, or reverence and awe, which is due to an important authority. Does the rest of the text support this interpretation of the theme of fear in this passage? This can be answered only by examining the whole context of the passage contained within these two exhortations "to fear."

The participle "submissive" is first applied to the wives, who are to be submissive to their own husbands. The translations that simply mention "husbands" miss the nuance of "your own" (*idiois*), which stands in distinction to being submitted to someone else's husband. This submission is modeled on that which every Christian owes to the Lord (v. 21), which is reinforced by the comparison of Christ, the head of the Church, to the husband, a comparison rooted in two biblical traditions.

THE ADULTERY-AND-PAROUSIA LINK

Different stages of understanding the consequences for sexual sins can be characterized in part by the levels of understanding life after death in Israel. In its earliest history, Israel did not speculate much on the afterlife, since that had been a preoccupation of Egypt, the place of their former slavery. The general sense in Israel's first centuries was that a person's name lived on after death through children, who remembered the names of the forebears. Based on this assumption, a wife who committed adultery (and her paramour) received the death penalty because her husband could not be sure if the children were his (DNA and blood typology were not yet invented), thereby jeopardizing his life after death. Whereas, if a husband had relations outside the marriage, he committed an offense, but not a capital crime, since his wife would still be assured of her children and their remembrance of her after death.

After the Babylonian Exile, some prophets — Ezekiel and Daniel — and other writings spoke of the resurrection of the dead. Jesus taught

continued on next page...

the same to his disciples. Life after death was not simply in the remembrance by children; rather, God would raise the dead to eternal life and reward — or punish each person into eternity. With this revelation came the understanding that both husbands and wives were equally responsible for sexual morality before God's judgment seat. Adultery and even lust can get either one into hell (Mt 5:27-28), while sexual responsibility in marriage is a sign of Jesus' union with the Church at the end of time (Eph 5:32; Rev 19:7-8).

Given this background, it is no surprise that St. Paul's teaching on marriage is affected by his expectation of the Parousia: in 1 Corinthians 7, his teaching hinges on the expectation of Christ's imminent return; in Ephesians, the immediacy of the return is not brought up, and living marriage in holiness is a more fully developed idea.

INVESTIGATE

MARRIAGE AS METAPHOR

 In the writings of the Old Testament prophets, the Lord God is the spouse of Israel, while in the New Testament, Jesus saw himself as a bridegroom. Look up the following passages and jot down how marriage is seen as a metaphor for God's/Jesus' relationship with Israel/the Church.

PASSAGE	NOTES
Hosea 1-3	
Jeremiah 3	
Ezekiel 16, 23	

Matthew 9:15	
Matthew 22:1-14	
Matthew 25:1-13	
Mark 2:19	
Revelation 19:1-9	
Revelation 21:1-7	
Revelation 21:9-14	

St. Paul's comparison of Christ to a bridegroom belongs to this important stream of biblical tradition.

Beyond the link with this biblical tradition — Ephesians 5:23-24, 31 — a new level of meaning is given to Paul's understanding of the Church as the Body of Christ. Keeping in mind that Genesis 2:24 teaches that the man and the woman become one flesh, it is possible to see the Church as the Body of Christ in the sense that the Church is the Bride of Christ, who has mystically become one flesh with him. This nuance helps preserve the distinction between Christ, the eternal Son of God become flesh, and his Body, the Church, with whom he is in a profound union. This aspect also points to an important theological meaning of marriage: the Sacrament of Matrimony becomes a profound sign of the loving commitment of Jesus the Lord to the Church. This sign elevates marital fidelity in a lifelong covenant to a profound mystery of faith (Eph 5:32).

St. Paul develops this insight as he addresses husbands about their manner of submitting to their wives. First, he points out that their love of their wives must be modeled on that of Christ's love for the Church. Because of this love, he handed himself over to death: "God shows his love for us in that while we were yet sinners Christ died for us" (Rom 5:8). At the Last Supper, Jesus told his disciples the same meaning of his death: "Greater love has no man than this, that a man lay down his life for his friends" (Jn 15:13). Given this understanding of Christ being a model of handing himself over to death out of love for his bride, the headship of the husband in the family means that he is to be enthroned upon a cross, always willing to give himself, even his own life, to save his wife and family. Normally, this occurs in the daily self-giving and dying to self, though throughout history this willingness to self-sacrifice has often turned deadly for husbands.

St. Paul further develops what it means for Christ to save the Church by connecting Christ's self-offering in death to Baptism (Eph 5:26-27). The purpose of Christ's death was to make the Church holy and clean from sin. The means by which he continues to do this is the washing of water through the word — Baptism. Note here, too, the connection with the form of the sacrament (the word of God, which is the formula for the sacrament) and the matter, which is the washing with water. Just as Paul connects Baptism with Jesus' death and resurrection in Romans 6:1-14 and Colossians 2:11-15, so he does here. Since Baptism flows from Christ's saving death, it has the power to make the Church "holy and blameless," a bride who lives in a way that is appropriate for her holy spouse, Jesus. Similarly, husbands love their wives as their own bodies, seeking their sanctification and the beauty of a blameless life. Clearly marriage is a "great mystery" that surpasses happiness on the natural level and is oriented to the very salvation of the husbands' and wives' souls.

DISCUSS

1. How is St. Paul's teaching on marriage in 1 Corinthians molded by his belief in the imminent return of Jesus? Does his focus change in later letters when it seems that Christ's coming may be delayed? What is the importance of celibacy within the Church?

2. How is the Sacrament of Matrimony a sign of the end of the world? How is celibacy a complementary sign of the end of the world?

3. How is marriage a symbol of Christ's relationship with the Church? How does St. Paul say a husband and wife should act toward each other in this regard?

4. What are the roles of a husband and wife, as St. Paul explains in his letters? What does he mean when he says that a spouse's faith might save the other?

5. How is marriage a mystery?

PRACTICE

What can you do to encourage young people to consider Matrimony as a sacred vocation? How would you consider explaining the importance of this vocation within the Church?

CONCLUSION

This book does not treat the Sacrament of the Anointing of the Sick because St. Paul does not mention it in his writings. Certainly his prayers for the sick and the laying on of hands led to a number of healings in the Acts of the Apostles, but he is never portrayed as having administered the Sacrament of the Sick, nor does he ever write about it. Therefore, we will pass over it in silence.

After having covered the passages where St. Paul teaches about six of the seven sacraments throughout his epistles, two general conclusions are warranted.

First, the centrality of the death and resurrection of Jesus Christ lies behind the mysteries of the sacraments. St. Paul is one of the New Testament writers to highlight this point, though others certainly teach it. His writings are a way to meditate on Jesus Christ crucified and risen from the dead, as we contemplate each sacrament.

St. Paul takes us into the central mystery of the sacraments so that we never lose sight of the person of Jesus Christ when we receive them. We never reduce them to mere human realities by turning them into human customs akin to some ancient magic. Rather, we see that the deepest human level of each sacrament derives from the profession of faith that Jesus Christ is God, who truly became flesh and died in a most human way. But because of that divinity, he also raised up and glorified that humanity in a true resurrection from the dead. He offers human beings the opportunities to enter into these mysteries through the sacraments.

Each sacrament unites the Christian believer with Jesus Christ, with his death and resurrection, so as to transform the believer. They help conform the life of the Christian to Jesus' own life, because, truly, God's grace is given to those who receive these sacraments. The graces are not amorphous, but instead they take shape within each sacrament, accomplishing the distinctive transformations proper to each one — Baptism, Confirmation, the Eucharist, Holy Orders, Holy Matrimony, Penance, and the Anointing of the Sick.

A second important theme in St. Paul's teaching on the sacraments is their connection with the Church, the Body of Christ. The sacraments unite Christians to this one body (Eph 4:4-7). They offer us gifts that help define each person's role within the Body of Christ (1 Cor 12-14). The sacraments manifest Christ's love for his body, the Church (Eph 5:21-33).

Christians are not called to individualistic salvation but rather to interpersonal communion with God and with the whole Church. The sacraments are always mysteries that engage us in these communions with God and with the Church here and now, so as to prepare us for the self-giving and for the acceptance of others that will continue for all eternity in heaven. St. Paul was a steward of these mysteries throughout his apostolic mission. He taught us about these mysteries throughout his epistles. Now we must take up the mysteries in our own lifetime, in accordance with the vocation each one has been given by God, and continue being stewards of these same mysteries.

Appendix

READING CHECKLIST

For the Jubilee Year of the Apostle Paul

The Year of St. Paul presents us with a unique opportunity to focus on the writings and teachings of the Apostle to the Gentiles. The following checklist is a suggested reading plan that you can use to read through all of St. Paul's letters in ninety-eight days and, as a bonus, the passages dealing with his life in the Acts of the Apostles in another thirty-six days.

1. ___ Romans 1		19. ___ Romans 15:14-33	
2. ___ Romans 2:1-3:8		20. ___ Romans 16	
3. ___ Romans 3:9-31		21. ___ 1 Corinthians 1	
4. ___ Romans 4		22. ___ 1 Corinthians 2	
5. ___ Romans 5		23. ___ 1 Corinthians 3	
6. ___ Romans 6		24. ___ 1 Corinthians 4	
7. ___ Romans 7		25. ___ 1 Corinthians 5	
8. ___ Romans 8:1-17		26. ___ 1 Corinthians 6	
9. ___ Romans 8:18-39		27. ___ 1 Corinthians 7:1-24	
10. ___ Romans 9:1-29		28. ___ 1 Corinthians 7:25-40	
11. ___ Romans 9:30-10:13		29. ___ 1 Corinthians 8	
12. ___ Romans 10:14-21		30. ___ 1 Corinthians 9	
13. ___ Romans 11:1-16		31. ___ 1 Corinthians 10:1-13	
14. ___ Romans 11:17-36		32. ___ 1 Corinthians 10:14-11:1	
15. ___ Romans 12		33. ___ 1 Corinthians 11:2-16	
16. ___ Romans 13		34. ___ 1 Corinthians 11:17-34	
17. ___ Romans 14		35. ___ 1 Corinthians 12	
18. ___ Romans 15:1-13		36. ___ 1 Corinthians 13	

37. ___ 1 Corinthians 14:1-25

38. ___ 1 Corinthians 14:26-40

39. ___ 1 Corinthians 15:1-34

40. ___ 1 Corinthians 15:35-58

41. ___ 1 Corinthians 16

42. ___ 2 Corinthians 1:1-22

43. ___ 2 Corinthians 1:23-2:17

44. ___ 2 Corinthians 3

45. ___ 2 Corinthians 4:1-15

46. ___ 2 Corinthians 4:16-5:17

47. ___ 2 Corinthians 5:18-7:1

48. ___ 2 Corinthians 7:2-16

49. ___ 2 Corinthians 8

50. ___ 2 Corinthians 9

51. ___ 2 Corinthians 10

52. ___ 2 Corinthians 11:1-21

53. ___ 2 Corinthians 11:22-33

54. ___ 2 Corinthians 12

55. ___ 2 Corinthians 13

56. ___ Galatians 1

57. ___ Galatians 2

58. ___ Galatians 3:1-4:7

59. ___ Galatians 4:8-31

60. ___ Galatians 5

61. ___ Galatians 6

62. ___ Ephesians 1

63. ___ Ephesians 2

64. ___ Ephesians 3

65. ___ Ephesians 4:1-16

66. ___ Ephesians 4:17-5:21

67. ___ Ephesians 5:22-6:9

68. ___ Ephesians 6:10-24

69. ___ Philippians 1

70. ___ Philippians 2

71. ___ Philippians 3:1-4:1

72. ___ Philippians 4:2-23

73. ___ Colossians 1

74. ___ Colossians 2

75. ___ Colossians 3

76. ___ Colossians 4

77. ___ 1 Thessalonians 1

78. ___ 1 Thessalonians 2

79. ___ 1 Thessalonians 3

80. ___ 1 Thessalonians 4

81. ___ 1 Thessalonians 5

82. ___ 2 Thessalonians 1

83. ___ 2 Thessalonians 2

84. ___ 2 Thessalonians 3

85. ___ 1 Timothy 1

86. ___ 1 Timothy 2

87. ___ 1 Timothy 3

88. ___ 1 Timothy 4

89. ___ 1 Timothy 5

90. ___ 1 Timothy 6

91. ___ 2 Timothy 1

92. ___ 2 Timothy 2

93. ___ 2 Timothy 3

94. ___ 2 Timothy 4

95. ___ Titus 1

96. ___ Titus 2

97. ___ Titus 3

98. ___ Philemon

BONUS

St. Paul in the Acts of the Apostles

99. ___ Acts 6

100. ___ Acts 7:1-22

101. ___ Acts 7:23-43

102. ___ Acts 7:44-8:2

103. ___ Acts 8:3-25

104. ___ Acts 8:26-40

105. ___ Acts 9:1-20

106. ___ Acts 9:21-43

107. ___ Acts 10:1-24

108. ___ Acts 11

109. ___ Acts 12

110. ___ Acts 13:1-25

111. ___ Acts 13:26-52

112. ___ Acts 14:1-15:5

113. ___ Acts 15:6-21

114. ___ Acts 15:22-41

115. ___ Acts 16:1-21

116. ___ Acts 16:22-40

117. ___ Acts 17:1-15

118. ___ Acts 17:16-34

119. ___ Acts 18

120. ___ Acts 19:1-20

121. ___ Acts 19:21-40

122. ___ Acts 20:1-16

123. ___ Acts 20:17-38

124. ___ Acts 21:1-14

125. ___ Acts 21:15-36

126. ___ Acts 21:37-22:29

127. ___ Acts 22:30-23:10

128. ___ Acts 23:11-35

129. ___ Acts 24

130. ___ Acts 25

131. ___ Acts 26

132. ___ Acts 27:1-26

133. ___ Acts 27:27-44

134. ___ Acts 28

A PRAYER TO THE APOSTLE PAUL

Glorious St. Paul,
most zealous apostle,
martyr for the love of Christ,
give us a deep faith,
a steadfast hope,
a burning love for our Lord,
so that we can proclaim with you,
"It is no longer I who live, but Christ who lives in me."

Help us to become apostles,
serving the Church with a pure heart,
witnesses to her truth and beauty
amidst the darkness of our days.
With you we praise God our Father:
"To him be the glory, in the Church and in Christ,
now and for ever."
Amen.

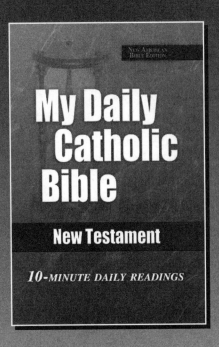
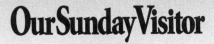